D1094008

I Believe in

JESUS CHRIST

I Believe in

JESUS
CHRIST

by Marbury E. Anderson
and Frank W. Klos

illustrated by Albert Michini

LUTHERAN CHURCH PRESS, PHILADELPHIA

LCA WEEKDAY CHURCH SCHOOL SERIES

Frank W. Klos, *Editor*

The head of Christ on the cover and the title page is adapted from a detail of Rembrandt's etching "Christ Healing the Sick" in the Metropolitan Museum of Art, New York.

Scripture quotations from the **Revised Standard Version** *of the Bible,* **copyrighted 1946 and 1952 by the Division of Christian Education, National Council of Churches, are used by permission.**

This pupil's book is accompanied by a teacher's guide, I Believe in Jesus Christ (WCS 8).

Did you know that almost two thousand years ago the name "Christian" was a dirty word? The people of Antioch who first used the word couldn't think of anything nastier to call the followers of the crucified carpenter from Galilee. But those who accepted Jesus as Lord of their lives bore the name proudly. As you read about their faith in Jesus Christ, you will be thinking seriously about what Jesus means to you. Do you bear his name proudly?

about this book

The term "Lutheran" was a nasty label, too. In the early part of the sixteenth century, anyone who supported the Wittenberg professor, Martin Luther, in his effort to purify the church was contemptuously called a "Lutheran." Yet, over the years that have passed since Luther nailed his ninety-five theses on the Castle Church door, a great many people have gladly and willingly accepted that name with pride. Like Luther, they believe that only in Jesus Christ does life have any meaning, only in him does God's forgiveness of our sins make any sense, and only in him does the love and presence of God himself seem real. You will be reading about Martin Luther's portrait of Christ. You will be questioning whether or not this German reformer has helped you understand Jesus more fully and accept him as your Lord more completely. Maybe you will also be willing to be labeled a Lutheran, willing and glad to bear that name with pride.

During this course, when you are probing the significance of Christ in your life, remember that your church is not interested in giving you a lot of trite answers to your questions about being good, about life, death, and eternity. Instead, your church wants you to read, study, and think for yourself, to let the Holy Spirit so increase your faith in Christ that you will find those answers that are meaningful to your life.

5

contents

Page

About This Book 5

Part One: God's Orderly World

1. *A Question for Everyone* . . 9
2. *"I Belong"* 12
3. *Law and Life* 15
4. *God's Law and the Ten Commandments* 20
5. *"I Am the Lord Your God"* 27

Part Two: Our Relationship with God

6. *God Comes First* 33
7. *God's Name Is Holy* 40
8. *Honoring the Word of God* 46

Part Three: Our Relationships with Others

9. *You and Your Family* . . . 54
10. *Respect for Human Life* . . 61
11. *The Holiness of Sex* 67
12. *Caring for Possessions* . . . 72
13. *Speaking the Truth in Love* 76

Part Four: God Expects Obedience

14. *Controlling Desires* 83
15. *"The Cord That Ties the Wreath Together"* 90

A Portfolio of Pictures of Christ 96

Page

Part Five: Our Greatest Need

16. Sinners Need a Savior 109
17. Peter's Experiences with
    Christ 112

Part Six: Jesus Christ Is My Lord

18. Jesus Christ Is True God .. 119
19. Jesus Christ Is True Man .. 123
20. Important Days in Jesus'
    Life 128
21. Christ, the Savior of the
    World 133
22. From Christ's Easter to
    Your Easter 138
23. "I Believe" 144

Part Seven: Luther's Discovery of Christ

24. The Law Student Who
    Became a Monk 149
25. "Here I Stand" 155
26. The Reformer at Work ... 162
27. Your Lutheran Heritage .. 169

Part Eight: The New Life in Christ

28. The Power of Love 173
29. Forgiveness 180
30. Living with a Thankful
    Heart 186

The Small Catechism by Martin
Luther, in Contemporary
English 193

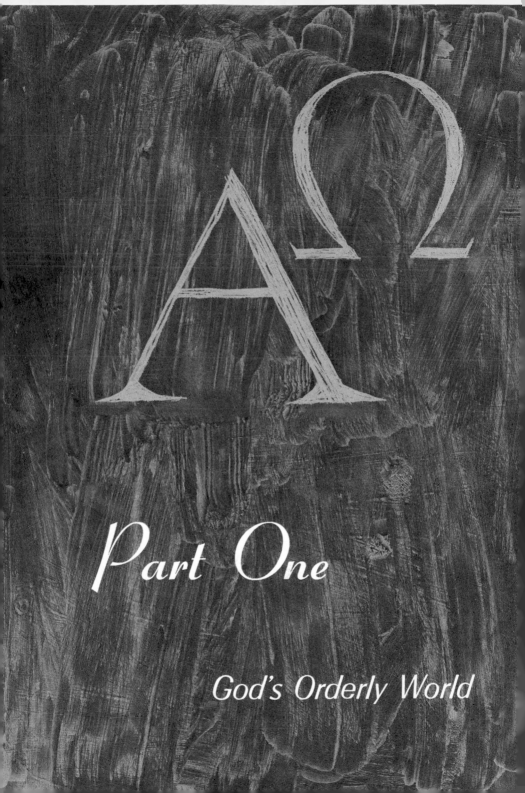

Part One

God's Orderly World

1

A QUESTION FOR EVERYONE

Who are you?

That's about the hardest question you will ever have to answer.

You could say, "I am Bill Smith of Oil City, Pennsylvania," or "Nancy Jones of Ottawa, Ontario." Fine! You've told us your identification tag and where you live. You could add, "I am thirteen and in the eighth grade." Now we know how old you are and where you are in school.

But who are you? What makes you tick? Isn't getting to know you much more than knowing a few facts about you?

Some people write autobiographies. They let people peek over their shoulders as they relate the interesting experiences they have had. Your life story may not seem particularly exciting and dramatic to you. On the other hand, it could be interesting to others—because you are you.

Every person is different. Twins may look alike and act alike. Yet even they are individuals. When God created people he didn't use a mold; he made each person unique. You can write an autobiography knowing that it will be unlike anyone else's life story.

you and other people

Though you are different from everyone else, you are also like everyone else in many ways. For this you can be thankful. A doctor can treat you when you are sick because your body is generally like the bodies of others. The grocer can stock his shelves with food you like because he knows you need and like much the same food that others do.

Being like others gives you a feeling of oneness with them. You learn to enjoy the many possible varieties among human beings. Each new acquaintance can be an exciting new experience. You like people; you want other people to like you. Isn't it true that when you are with people you like you are happy? But isn't it also true that sometimes you are very unhappy?

Remember the party where you had so much fun? Remember also the party to which you weren't invited? Did you ever join a club and discover the others in the club were doing things of which you did not approve? Strange, isn't it? People can make you so happy; but they can also make you feel miserable. Sometimes your closest friends are so good to you; at other times they can be so annoying or unkind.

You are not the only one who feels this way; other people have the same experiences. You've noticed the ways your friends react to you. At times, you've been able to do so much for them. At other times, everything you've done has seemed to go wrong. Others get in your way and you get in their way.

It's a crazy world. You need others; they need you. You enjoy others; they enjoy you. Yet you sometimes fight with them and they fight with you. This is when trying to live harmoniously with others becomes a real problem. You have guilty feelings; but usually they do, too. You aren't sure what to think. They are a threat to you and you are a threat to them. Sometimes you spin in a whirl of worry. You wonder why life has to be this way. Why is life so mixed up at times? Why can't we all be happy all the time?

a clue from the bible

The answer to our question about being happy all the time is as old as the Book of Genesis. Read the first three chapters. Here are graphic stories of man and woman created by God to live in the orderly world he made for them. Everything was the way it should be; there was no discord. These two enjoyed each other's company. They knew God and were close to him. God told them, "Be fruitful and multiply, and fill the earth and subdue it; and have dominion over the fish of the sea and over the birds of the air and over every living thing that moves upon the earth" (Genesis 1:28).

But things did not stay perfect, as you know. They did not stay perfect because the man and woman decided to do what God had told them not to do.

The fact that they "decided" is important. One of the things that sets man apart from every other living thing is his ability to think for himself, to decide what he wants to do with his life. This freedom of choice is God's gift. You aren't like the rest of the animal kingdom over which you "have dominion"; you are the special creation of God, placed in a role of great importance and special concern. You are a responsible, creative, free human being.

The stories in Genesis show clearly that men can turn against God; that they can make wrong choices; that they can ignore God's will for them; that they can fail to trust God completely. For instance, Adam and Eve did precisely what God told them not to do. But why did they eat the forbidden fruit? There were plenty of other fruit-bearing trees in the Garden. Actually, the fruit itself wasn't important. They wanted something else. The words of the serpent, who represents temptation, planted a new desire in their minds. "You will not die. For God knows that when you eat of it (the fruit) your eyes will be opened, and you will be like God, knowing good and evil" (Genesis 3:4-5).

10

In the Genesis stories, sin was born when Adam and Eve turned against God. They weren't satisfied to be creatures of God, to live obediently and contentedly under his guidance. They wanted to be like God, to have his power. They wanted to take all of life into their own hands and do whatever they wanted with it. Instead of following God's will, they rebelled and chose to follow their own desires. In selfishness and outright disobedience, they did the wrong thing.

The serenity of their happiness was shattered. God was going one way, but they were going another. The earthly paradise was destroyed. Before long, the sinfulness of Adam and Eve infected one of their sons, Cain—and Cain, in jealous anger, killed his brother. Turning against God's will has a contagious quality: Sin is a disease that spreads from generation to generation.

Sin has a way of corrupting happiness and destroying contentment. Adam and Eve wanted to hide from God; they were embarrassed in his presence. They felt his displeasure and anger. But they couldn't honestly face the truth about themselves. So they dreamed up alibis and blamed each other for their acts of disobedience. By their own free will, they had turned the Garden of Eden into a place of work and pain, of suffering and death.

The creation stories of Genesis are a form of holy history. In them, you can see yourself as you really are. You know that God has created you, that he wants you on this earth, that he provides for your needs. But you also know that, like the first men and all men, you often turn against God and insist on having your own way. Sin is really saying "No" to God. The Old Testament prophets frequently spoke of sinfulness as "hardheartedness." When they said someone had a hard heart, they meant that he did not want to be touched or changed or guided by God. He wanted to live his life alone, so he shut his heart to God's will.

back to our question

"Who are you?" You can find the answer in the story of the first man and woman. You are created by God for a rich and satisfying life with him. But, like Adam and Eve, you have difficulty surrendering your own free will to God. You, too, feel separated from God when you sin. You, too, have feelings of guilt and at times would hide from God if you could. Isn't it true that you and your Creator are often out of step with each other?

"Who are you?" No one can be satisfied with saying, "I am a person out of step with God." How do you get in step again?

2

"I BELONG"

Every human being needs a sense of belonging; no one is really happy by himself. For this reason your family is important to you. You may get irked at many things in your family life, but deep down inside you want to be a part of your family. You want to know that the welcome mat is always out on the doorstep for you at home.

TO READ AND THINK ABOUT

Matthew 14:13-21	Feeding the Five Thousand
Matthew 15:21-28	The Canaanite Woman
Matthew 17:14-20	Power in Faith
Matthew 18:1-14	The Greatest
Matthew 18:21-35	Forgiven and Forgiving
Matthew 19:16-24	The Needle's Eye
Matthew 20:20-34	Two Requests

Have you ever been with people and felt that somehow you didn't belong? Maybe you went visiting with your parents to a strange house. You felt out of place, uncomfortable. How you wanted to be back home!

Or maybe a friend said he was going somewhere and you went along. When you arrived you discovered that you were an "extra"; it was no fun. You felt like a harmonica player at a violinists' convention.

Everyone wants to belong, to feel wanted and liked for himself, to be an important part of his group. You want this feeling of belonging not only at home and with your friends, but at school, on the ball field, in church.

you belong to God

Do you ever feel uncomfortable when you think about your relationship to God? Usually this feeling comes when you are aware that you are a sinner, that you aren't always the kind of person God wants you to be, that you are out of step with him. You know you should do things that you don't do. You also know that you do things you shouldn't do. Maybe you think that because you have turned against God's will so many times he is more likely to be a foe than a friend.

Other people have felt this way. When the prophet Isaiah was a young man he saw the Lord in the Temple. Suddenly he heard the angelic beings, the seraphim, singing to one another, "Holy, holy, holy is the LORD of hosts; the whole earth is full of his glory." Isaiah felt uncomfortable in the midst of this great experience. He felt that he didn't really belong. "Woe is me!" he said. "For I am lost; for I am a man of unclean lips, and I dwell in the midst of a people of unclean lips . . ." (Isaiah 6:5).

Have you ever tried to hide from God or to tell him to leave you alone? Have you ever assumed that because you are guilty of sinning against him he will have nothing more to do with you?

This isn't the way God wants his relationship with you to be. He may not like some of the things you do, but he loves you. He created you, and he provides for your daily needs because he loves you. He wants you to live with him in this life and in the life to come. He knows you cannot battle your sinfulness all by yourself. God, in his great wisdom, sees your every need. That is why he sent his Son Jesus Christ into the world to help you. God never wants you to forget that, no matter what happens, you still belong to him and he still loves you.

John 3:16 has often been called "the gospel in miniature." In just one sentence, it explains God's concern for every person: "For God so loved the world that he gave his only Son, that whoever believes in him should not perish but have eternal life." The only way you can prevent God's gifts of love and forgiveness from helping you is by denying the power of his Son. Yes, you can reject Christ as your personal Savior. You can do it because God has given you the freedom to decide what you want to do with your life. But even if you do, you will never escape God's call to accept Jesus as your Lord. So great is God's love for you that he will never stop telling you that you are his child.

life's greatest discovery

Your greatest discovery in life is that Jesus Christ is your Lord. He makes it possible for you to continue belonging to the family of God. Jesus Christ helps you to know who you really are—a sinner, yes, but also a son of God who can walk with him.

To study the life and teachings of Jesus Christ is tremendously exciting. Through Christ, you become better acquainted with yourself; you stop being a stranger whom you don't understand. You begin to see that God intends you to live a happy, creative life in close, friendly association with him and with other people. Because of Christ and his love for you, your sins are forgiven. He can give you the strength to handle temptations and the guidance you need for your worries and problems.

When you were baptized, the pastor asked your parents, "Do you believe in Jesus Christ, his only Son our Lord, Who was conceived by the Holy Ghost, Born of the Virgin Mary, Suffered under Pontius Pilate, Was crucified, dead, and buried: Descended into hell; The third day rose again from the dead; Ascended into heaven, And sitteth on the right hand of God the Father Almighty; Whence he shall come to judge the quick and the dead?"

They answered, "I believe" to the questions concerning this and the other articles of the Apostles' Creed. Then they were asked, "Do you present *this Child* to be baptized into this Christian Faith?" They answered, "I do."

Then the pastor baptized you "In the Name of the Father, and of the Son, and of the Holy Ghost," putting water on your head to illustrate God's cleansing power. Christian baptism is a way of letting the whole world know that you, and every other baptized Christian, belong to God.

You became a member of the Christian church the day you were baptized. This is because you belong to God, and therefore you also belong to the family of God, to his church. On confirmation day you will be professing your personal faith before the congregation. The pastor will ask you if you believe in God, in Jesus Christ, in the Holy Spirit. You and the other members of your class will answer, repeating each of the articles of the Apostles' Creed. The congregation then will welcome you to participate in the Sacrament of the Altar. In this sacrament, Jesus Christ will be coming to you, continually offering his forgiveness, strength, and power. He will be helping you to know again and again who you are, to know that you belong to God.

3
LAW AND LIFE

When you have a close relationship with someone, like a friend, you know that he usually expects you to act a certain way when you are with him. Your parents make it clear that you are to live a certain way around the house. They ask you to develop manners at mealtime, to take responsibility for some household duties, to keep yourself and your possessions orderly and neat. They also depend on you to be a credit to them when you are away from home, so they give you a lot of rules to follow. When you have matured enough to understand that you have a special relationship with God, that you belong to him as his child, you begin to realize that he, too, expects much from you wherever you are.

TO READ AND THINK ABOUT
Psalm 1:1-3   Living by God's Law
Psalm 19:7-10   God's Law Is Perfect
Psalm 119:161-168   Love of God's Law
Matthew 5:17-20   Jesus and the Law
Matthew 22:36-40   Two Great Commandments
Deuteronomy 6:4-9   Love Your God
Leviticus 19:17-18   Love Your Neighbor

Gift shops often sell little painted signs that you can hang on the walls of your room. One of these signs says, "Everything I like is either illegal, immoral, or fattening." Maybe you feel this way sometimes. Everywhere you turn there are laws, rules, regulations telling you what you can and what you cannot do. It seems as if you can seldom do what you want to do. Sometimes you feel as frustrated as the boy who cut neighbors' lawns in order to earn money to buy skin-diving equipment. When he arrived at the state park lake, loaded down with mask, snorkel, and flippers, he saw a sign: "Positively no underwater swimming equipment allowed."

laws are necessary

The budding skin diver complained to a lifeguard about the strictness of the "no underwater equipment" rule. He soon found out that the law was necessary. Several people using underwater gear had already drowned in the lake. The lifeguards on duty had enough to do just keeping a careful lookout for the safety of those who were swimming on the water's surface. The park authorities were not trying to be mean; they just wanted to protect swimmers from harm.

Many man-made laws, whether they are made by park authorities or by city and national governments, are designed for your protection. Think of the stoplight that regulates the flow of traffic so that you can walk across a busy street. Think of the laws controlling the purity of the milk you drink, so that you can be sure that you will not get a disease.

Laws help us live peacefully with one another with a minimum of danger. It is a good feeling to know that there are policemen and other law enforcement officials to make sure that laws are obeyed.

Laws are necessary to help regulate the way we live so there will be little confusion and uncertainty. Your school has a series of laws telling you exactly what to do during a fire drill. If the school ever caught fire, you would know exactly how to get to safety. First-aid methods insist that you follow a certain pattern of administering treatment. If you are ever called upon in an emergency, then you will do the right thing automatically. Even games need their specific rules. Wouldn't it be confusing if every ball park had its own baseball regulations? A home run on one field could be an automatic out somewhere else. Your favorite big league team would have a terrible time trying to play the other teams in the league. Think of the problems of running a World Series.

Even tax laws are necessary if a community is to provide for the needs of all its citizens. Ball fields and schools, parks and highways cost a lot of money; it is only right that every person who is financially able should pay his share.

When you stop and think about it, most of the laws that we have were made by people who had to obey those laws, too. Therefore, they must have felt that laws were not only necessary for orderliness in the world, but good to have.

natural laws

In addition to man-made laws that govern our actions, there are also natural laws that control our physical world. Natural laws are what we call the happenings in nature that are orderly and regular. God built order and consistency right into the very structure of the universe that he created. Natural laws guide the flow of the seasons and determine daily balance of day and night. There is a certain dependability about the world. Water always flows downhill; trees grow up.

The so-called laws of nature cannot be ignored. You can take a chance and walk along the crumbly rim of the Grand Canyon, if you want to. But if your foot slips, the law of gravity is going to take over no matter how much you wish it wouldn't.

16

Health and disease both operate by natural laws. You learn good health laws so that you can keep your body and mind working well. You have to eat the right food and get proper amounts of rest and exercise in order to stay at the peak of condition. Even a simple matter like brushing your teeth regularly is mighty important if you want to keep your own teeth for many years to come. Sometimes you have to go through the agony of a fierce toothache before you realize that your health depends on your good health habits.

While God made natural laws a very important part of his world, he didn't tell men about them. Wisely, he allowed men to discover the benefit of these laws as they are capable of understanding them.

Sometimes man stumbled accidentally on a natural law. Perhaps one day a long time ago, lightning struck a fallen tree, setting it on fire and roasting an animal caught in its tangled branches. Some primitive man tasted the cooked meat and discovered that it was good. As our friend lingered by the smoldering wood to continue his meal he felt very comfortable in the heat. He found out that wood burns, fire warms, fire makes meat better to eat.

Sometimes natural laws are newly discovered through scientific investigation, and the old understanding of laws is revised. Each year of our atomic era brings new insights into the nature of our marvelous, orderly universe. There is no end in sight to what we can learn about the natural forces operating in our corner of space.

God's laws

In order to feel at home in their world, people need more than an understanding of the orderliness of their physical surroundings, more than the man-made laws they develop to regulate their lives. They need to know how to live in their relationships with God and with other people. They want guidance in how to think and what to feel as well as direction in how to act.

God knows our every need and provides the answer. He reveals his will to us; he tells us what he expects of us. He has given us laws to govern our important relationships in life so that we can live happily with him and contentedly with each other.

The laws God gave directly to men are very old. They can be traced back to the dim beginnings of the Hebrew people, when God took the descendants of Abraham and established a special relationship with them. He revealed his dependable, abiding love for men and wanted the Hebrews to set an example of righteous living for all other peoples of the world to follow. God spoke to his chosen people through their great leaders like Abraham and Moses, through their prophets like Amos and Isaiah. In time the laws he had set forth for his people were written down as part of various books. Much later the books were collected and put together as part of the Old Testament.

Some of the laws were ceremonial laws telling the Hebrews how to develop their worship practices; some were health laws designed to keep the people in good physical condition. There were even laws to help the Hebrews establish and run their nation. Most of these laws were special laws for a people living under primitive conditions at a certain period in history. But God also gave his people timeless moral laws that apply to all people everywhere and demand their obedience.

When Jesus came, preaching the gospel of God's saving love, there were many who thought that he was doing away with God's Law. Jesus set them straight. "Think not that I have come to abolish the law and the prophets," said Jesus. "I have come not to abolish them but to fulfil them." He also pointed out, "Whoever then relaxes one of the least of these commandments and teaches men so, shall be called least in the kingdom of heaven; but he who does them and teaches them shall be called great in the kingdom of heaven" (Matthew 5:17,19).

The Christian church, guided by the Holy Spirit, has always felt that those moral laws of God such as the Ten Commandments, which govern all of sinful mankind, are to be obeyed. But those laws which are peculiar to the Jewish people in their ritual and political affairs are not binding on Christians.

The church teaches, too, that the way we fulfill these moral laws is important. Jesus made this clear: "I tell you, unless your righteousness exceeds that of the scribes and Pharisees, you will never enter the kingdom of heaven" (Matthew 5:20). He meant that merely keeping the letter of the law is not enough. We must do it willingly and gladly, because we love God and our fellowmen. That is what is important to God.

excuses

Our whole life, as well as the world we live in, is shaped and colored by law. Everywhere you turn there are laws of God and laws of men to follow. Do you ever wish that you could have some handy excuses to use so that you could live the way you want to?

How about the excuse called "Everybody's doing it"? When you use this excuse you can do a lot of things that down deep in your heart you know are wrong. No one really likes to be alone, to go against the wishes of the crowd. You want to do what your gang does; otherwise they might think you aren't friendly. You want to follow the customs and practices of your community; or else people might look at you as some kind of outcast. The trouble with this excuse is that it makes you afraid to do what you know is right. You are no longer a free, independent person who can think for himself; you become a slave to the pressures any group puts on you.

There is an excuse called "I need to do (or need to have) that in order to be happy." Your happiness is important, isn't it? So it doesn't matter how you do what you want to do or get what you want to have; even if you break a few laws in the process, you deserve happiness. The only trouble is that happiness is a fleeting thing. Just when you pounce on it and grab it and think you have it, it disappears. Often a child at Christmas, who finds under his tree everything he asked Santa Claus to bring, discovers that he still isn't satisfied. So he starts a new list of things he would like to have.

Another popular excuse is labeled "What I do is my own business." Using this excuse presumes that you have no obligation to anyone else. You are your own boss. The only trouble with this excuse is that the more you use it the more lonely you become. You are isolating yourself, cutting yourself off from everyone else, even from God at times.

Maybe you would like to try your hand at naming some of the other familiar excuses people use when they know they are breaking laws. Maybe you have used some of them yourself, especially when you tried to explain why you were not doing what was expected of you. Call them excuses, explanations, reasons—call them whatever you like, but aren't they really escape routes from responsibility for our ways of thinking and acting?

When we are honest with ourselves, we realize how frequently we do sin and fall far short of being the kind of persons God intended us to be. How can we overcome these sinful tendencies and obey God's laws? We need someone to help us.

the ministry of Jesus

Jesus came to be our helper. Through the perfect life he lived, through the way he loved both God and man, he fulfilled God's Law. He interpreted all of the Law in terms of love. He knew that no one could keep a set of rules perfectly. Therefore, his ministry to people was to give them a new heart which trusted God completely and loved others with a real concern for their well-being.

While he was in Jerusalem during the last week of his earthly life, Jesus met a young lawyer who asked him: "Teacher, which is the great commandment in the law?" Jesus answered quietly, "You shall love the Lord your God with all your heart, and with all your soul, and with all your mind. This is the great and first commandment." He paused and looked keenly at the lawyer. "And a second is like it," he went on. "You shall love your neighbor as yourself. On these two commandments depend all the law and the prophets" (Matthew 22:36-40).

Two great commandments! These Jesus followed. This was the way he fulfilled the Law; this is the way, too, he will help us live by God's will. With his power, he strengthens us in becoming new persons who want to make God's will our will.

4

GOD'S LAW AND THE TEN COMMANDMENTS

Members of a church in a small English town felt that the Ten Commandments were no longer meaningful to a Christian congregation. They decided to drop the use of the Commandments in their church services. The pastor of the church told a newspaper reporter, "The Commandments give a false impression, especially to young people, that religion is just a series of prohibitions." Maybe you feel this way, too.

TO READ AND THINK ABOUT

Exodus 20:1-17   The Giving of the Ten Commandments
Deuteronomy 5:6-21—Moses Lists God's Laws
Psalm 111:5-10   God's Wonderful Covenant
Jeremiah 31:31-34   The New Covenant
John 3:16-21   God's Gift of His Son
Matthew 26:26-28   The Last Supper
Romans 13:8-10   Love Is the Fulfilling of the Law

Despite the fact that Jesus said his mission was not to destroy the Law but to fulfill it, many people still feel that the laws of God, and in particular the Ten Commandments, are out of date. A lot has happened to the world since that ancient time when God gave the Ten Commandments to Moses on Mount Sinai. What has a world of astronauts and nuclear physics in common with a world of sheepherders and psalm writers?

The world certainly has changed in the thousands of years that have passed since the Commandments were introduced to the Hebrew people. It has changed considerably. But people themselves have not changed. The same crimes against God and against men are still going on. There are still those who believe that they are the very center of the universe and live accordingly. There are still those who rob or cheat or lie or kill to have their own way.

law comes from love

When you first started riding a bike, your dad may have given you a whole list of things you couldn't do. You couldn't "cowboy" your bike down the middle of the street; you couldn't ride a friend on the handlebars. Maybe you resented his interference with your fun. Or maybe you deliberately broke his rules when you knew he couldn't see you. But later on you came to realize that your dad insisted on these "laws" because he loved you. He loved you so much that he didn't want anything tragic to happen to you or to anyone else because of you. Now you accept his ideas and follow his guidance gladly. Bike safety is becoming second nature; it is part of the way you live. The rules are still there. But now you don't resent them. As a matter of fact, the rules are helpful; they let you check up on yourself to see if you are as careful a bike rider as you can be.

In much the same way we discover that God gives us his law because he loves us. He doesn't set up a whole list of restrictions just to put a wet blanket over all the things we want to do. He loves us and, therefore, he cares what happens to us. The more we accept him as the God of love, the more we realize how beneficial his laws really are. And as Jesus pointed out, you can summarize all of God's Commandments simply in terms of love of God and love of our fellowmen.

the mirror

Remember the wicked queen in the fairy tale about Snow White and the seven dwarfs? She owned a magic mirror that would answer truthfully any question she asked. Often she would say, "Mirror, mirror, on the wall, who is the fairest one of all?" The mirror usually answered, "You are"—that is, until the day that Snow White grew to be a beautiful young lady. In a certain sense the Ten Commandments, God's laws of love, are a kind of mirror that shows us ourselves as we really are. We may fool our friends or even our family into thinking that we are better people than we are. But we can't fool ourselves and we certainly can't fool God.

"You shall love" is always written above the image of ourselves in the mirror of the Commandments, challenging us, stabbing our consciences. Each commandment tells us what God expects of us as his people; each makes clear how he wants our love of him and our fellowmen to be translated into holy ways of living. It is here that we see ourselves as sinners unable to fulfill these demands.

As we look at the Ten Commandments, we realize how imperfect we are and how much we need the forgiveness God freely gives us in the name of Christ. We recognize our sinfulness: that we do not trust God completely as Jesus did nor do we love our fellowmen as he did. Each commandment is an example of the way love for God and for other people operates. We really need this honest look at ourselves before we can come to God in prayer. Then when we pray, when we realize our need of God's help, he gives it gladly. He sends us the Holy Spirit to guide our lips in prayer, to stimulate our willingness to grow in holiness. As Paul pointed out, "Likewise the Spirit helps us in our weakness; for we do not know how to pray as we ought, but the Spirit himself intercedes for us with sighs too deep for words" (Romans 8:26).

the club

Most policemen the world over carry some kind of club. The club is a symbol of the power a policeman has for use if necessary to enforce the laws. Some people are held in check from breaking the law when they see the club; it reminds them of the punishment in store for lawbreakers. In this sense, God uses his Law as a club to remind us of the punishments he has promised for wrongdoing. All people must realize that they are to live under God's rules, that he expects them to obey whether they like it or not. The Ten Commandments stand as a warning particularly to those who try to ignore God or who are indifferent to his requests or who refuse to discipline themselves. Make no mistake about it; God promises loneliness and misery to those who break his laws.

Even if a murderer escaped punishment by local government, he would not escape God. He still would stand liable for God's punishment. The terrible time for him will come when one day he comes into God's presence for judgment. If he has ignored God's laws and rejected Christ's offer of forgiveness, he has no defense.

The Ten Commandments are an example of one way God offers guidance to nations and people as they set up laws to govern themselves. He knows that they may have to use force and punishment to see that the laws are carried out, but this is the way it has to be. Human life must be protected and preserved if people are to live together contentedly, helping each other to have a full and satisfying life.

the new life in Christ

For the Christian, the Ten Commandments are an expression of God's will for his life. When you accept the fact that you belong to God when you accept Jesus Christ as your Lord, you no longer see the Commandments as a heavy club hanging over your head. Now, God's Law is an expression of the kind of person you want to be. You obey gladly and willingly. God does not have to compel you to fulfill his Commandments. Because you love him, you are quite happy to make his desires your desires.

But, you say, the Ten Commandments do not tell me what God's will is under all conditions. That is true. There are many areas of modern living that are not covered by them. The Commandments are not a complete book of rules that deal with every situation. They are not supposed to be. They are, when they are correctly understood, a brief description of the relationship a godly person has with

God and with his fellowmen. Living by God's will means letting God develop a Christlike personality within you. To be Christlike is to seek to do only that which helps other people, to seek to do only that which would make God proud of you.

Paul explains the new life in Christ by saying that, when we are Christians, we allow Christ to live within us. "I have been crucified with Christ," he wrote to the churches in Galatia, referring to the way God's forgiveness destroyed his sinfulness, "It is no longer I who live, but Christ who lives in me; and the life I now live in the flesh I live by faith in the Son of God, who loved me and gave himself for me" (Galatians 2:20).

In his famous list of Beatitudes, or blessings that the person who lives with God experiences, Jesus said, "Blessed are the pure in heart, for they shall see God." (Matthew 5:8) This purity of heart means single-mindedness in our attitude toward God; we want only to put him first in our life. It also means sincerity in desiring to do his will. To pray "Thy will be done," and to mean what we say, is a hard job. But then Jesus never said that discipleship was easy.

Each time we fail to make God's will our own, the Ten Commandments once more become a mirror to show us our sinfulness and a club to warn us of the consequences of disobedience.

the ten commandments and the covenant

The Jewish people not only saw the Ten Commandments as part of God's Law for them, but they also saw them as a sign of a *covenant* they had with God. A covenant is a formal, binding agreement between two parties. In ancient days when two kings signed a peace treaty between their kingdoms, they often drew up a covenant. This was an agreement saying what each king would or would not do for the other. A covenant was not a bargain, however, between two equals. One of the kings was usually stronger. Therefore, he set the terms of the covenant.

God made such a covenant with the Hebrews. He promised to be their God, to care for them, to give them a land to call their own. They, on their part, were to be his people and to live a godly life.

When you think of the Ten Commandments, you probably think of Moses. It was Moses to whom God gave the sign of this covenant in the form of the Ten Commandments on two tablets of stone. Why not read the story of this memorable event for yourself in Exodus 20? Incidentally, the Ten Commandments are also recorded in Deuteronomy 5. (Here Moses is addressing an assembly of his people, telling them what he heard on Mount Sinai.)

The Hebrews carried the stone tablets with them wherever they went on the rest of their journeys in the wilderness. Eventually, when they were settled down in the Promised Land, they put the tablets in the Holy of Holies (a special part of the temple). In this

way they would be reminded constantly of their part of their agreement with God. They knew that if they sinned against God by following their way instead of his they deserved punishment; they were breaking the covenant.

But no one was capable of keeping the Commandments perfectly. Neither could anyone really make up for his sins. When they had sinned, therefore, the Hebrews would offer sacrifices to God as gifts to make him forgive their wrongdoings. They would kill an animal from their flocks, or a bird, and hope that God would be pleased to accept the death of a perfect animal in place of the death of an imperfect person who deserved it.

There were some who believed that it didn't matter what they did contrary to God's wishes; they could always offer a nice fat lamb or a husky bull on the altar. As the blood of the animal ran over the stones, God would have to forgive them. At the other extreme, there were those who kept the very letter of the law and became so smug that they were hardly fit to live with. Their pride in their own accomplishments made them forget to live with a love of God and a love of their fellowmen in their hearts. Like little Jack Horner, they went around saying, "Oh, what a good boy am I."

the new covenant

God knew that his people did not keep their part of the covenant. He was pleased neither by routine sacrifices nor by those who prided themselves overmuch on keeping the Law. But this did not prevent him from seeking to help them, even at great cost to himself. He provided a *new covenant* under which they should live. In Jesus of Nazareth, God himself came down to men. He showed them how to live holy lives by giving them an example to follow. But more than that, as Jesus Christ he won a victory over all the forces of evil by his perfect love. Christ died on the cross as a perfect sacrifice of dedication. Here was a demonstration of God's love for his people. In the familiar words of John's Gospel, "For God sent the Son into the world, not to condemn the world, but that the world might be saved through him" (John 3:17). Through faith in Christ, men receive forgiveness of sin so that they can stand clean and pure in the presence of God. This great gift of God in Christ has made it possible for men to surrender their lives in faith, to say "Yes" to God's will, to know the joy and blessing of living holy lives.

The prophet Jeremiah knew long ago that the day of the new covenant was coming. Listen to what he told his fellow Hebrews: "But this is the covenant which I will make with the house of Israel . . . , says the LORD: I will put my law within them, and I will write it upon their hearts; and I will be their God, and they shall be my people." (Read Jeremiah 31:31-34 for more details of this wonderful message.)

If you think about this covenant idea, you can understand something of what Jesus was saying when he shared that last supper in the Upper Room with his disciples. While they were eating this simple meal to celebrate the Passover, Jesus took bread from the table and broke it and gave it to the disciples. "Take, eat," he said, "this is my body." And he took the cup of wine also from the table, again gave a prayer of thanks, and again gave it to the Twelve. "Drink of it, all of you," Jesus continued, "for this is my blood of the covenant, which is poured out for many for the forgiveness of sins" (Matthew 26:26-28).

In contrast to the sinful men who offered the blood of an animal on an altar to please God, Jesus offered his own life, his body and blood. He made the perfect sacrifice for all men for all time. All we have to do is take the gift of forgiveness that he offers so freely. This is the gospel, the good news that the New Testament proclaims with such power and joy. (The word "testament," by the way, is a translation of Bible words which mean "covenant." So, you see, the whole Bible is divided into the "Old" and the "New" ways of living with God.)

Only Jesus could live completely according to God's will; only Jesus could offer a perfect human life in dedication to God. Any man who accepts Jesus as his Lord will likewise have his marvelous relationship with God. This is because, in Christ, God forgives your sin, calls you to be his adopted son, and invites you to live by his will. He makes you an heir to all the gifts of eternity that he has prepared for those who give themselves to him.

the Christ-filled person

Being a Christian is being filled with Christ. It is learning to live with love in our hearts as he did. In this way, we learn to fulfill God's Commandments, for as Paul says, "Love is the fulfilling of the law" (Romans 13:10). The Ten Commandments, interpreted by the teachings of Christ, then become a description of the way we as Christians should live not only on Sundays and special holy days but every day. If you truly have Christ as your Lord, there is no other way.

5

"I AM THE LORD YOUR GOD"

As you turn to Exodus 20:2 or to Deuteronomy 5:6 to begin a careful study of the Ten Commandments, you will notice that they begin, "I am the LORD your God." This statement is an introduction to all of the Commandments which follow. This is the reason for there being Commandments in the first place. Because God made us, loves us, cares for us, he can tell us how he wants us to live. The only way we can really understand and accept the meaning of each commandment is to know God intimately as our heavenly Father.

TO READ AND THINK ABOUT

Psalm 100   The Lord Is God
Isaiah 40:9-11   Behold Your God
Psalm 46:8-11   Be Still and Know God
John 14:8-11   Christ Is God
Galatians 4:4-7   We Are God's Adopted Sons
Psalm 112:1-10   Delighting in His Commandments
Hebrews 12:7-11   God Disciplines His Sons

---

your God

The one great fact of this world is God. He fashioned the planets and the distant stars; he created life itself. But God didn't make the world like some kindly old clockmaker who makes a clock and starts it ticking, but then has nothing more to do with it. God is always active in this world, his world. He loves each person individually; he wants each person to live in fellowship with him forever. He is your God.

The Bible is really one long letter from God telling us how he cares for us and what he wants to do on our behalf. We belong to him. Listen to an unknown psalmist exult!

Know that the LORD is God!
  It is he that made us, and we are his;
   we are his people, and the sheep of his pasture.
            (Psalm 100:3)

For a long time, God spoke to his people through men like the psalmists and the prophets. But when his people paid little attention to those who were speaking for him, God himself came into the world. In Jesus, he was a baby, a child, a teen-ager, and adult. He lived through all human experiences so he could talk to men in their own language of understanding. He wanted them to know that they were likewise sons of God. Paul explained this dramatic act of God's coming into our world: "But when the time had fully come, God sent forth his Son, born of woman, born under the law, to redeem those who were under the law, so that we might receive adoption as sons" (Galatians 4:4-5).

God loves us so much that he wants us to be very close to him, like members of his own family. He wants us to know him personally, to talk to him intimately. Paul continues his explanation: "And because you are sons, God has sent the Spirit of his Son into our hearts, crying 'Abba! Father!' " (Galatians 4:6). This word "Abba" means something like "Daddy" or "Papa." In other words, Paul is saying that God is so close to us that we can talk to him in terms we only use with those who mean a lot to us. It was for this reason that Jesus taught us to pray, "Our Father, who art in heaven. . . ."

you are baptized

When God gave the Ten Commandments to his people, he began by introducing himself, "I am the LORD your God." Then he added, "who brought you out of the land of Egypt, out of the house of bondage." Because God had delivered the people of Israel from slavery, they were to recognize and accept him as their God. Therefore, they were to have no other gods, to honor God's name, to keep the Sabbath holy, and to fulfill all the other Commandments.

For the Christian, God's deliverance is from the slavery of sin rather than from bondage in Egypt. The Sacrament of Baptism demonstrates God's entering the Christian's life and freeing him from sin's control. In return for this deliverance, God expects the Christian to acknowledge him as the one, true, and holy God, and to live by the Commandments. Only when a Christian remembers that his baptism has linked him in love and trust to a loving God, does obeying God's Commandments make any sense.

Out on the western ranges in the springtime, ranchers round up the newly born calves and brand them with their particular mark. By looking at the brand a calf wears on his hide you can tell right away where he belongs. So in effect is God branding you with his mark at your baptism. There are no marks on your skin, however. As you grow up, the only way people can tell that God is your heavenly Father is by the way you live. If you have any doubts about who you are, remember that God has branded you; through Baptism he made you his child.

Martin Luther faced many difficulties in his stormy life. Sometimes he was faced with serious problems and he didn't know what to do about them. Sometimes he was plagued by temptations to do things that were wrong. But he found a way of handling these situations. When he got confused and didn't know which way to turn, he would say to himself simply, "I am baptized! I am baptized!" Over and over again he would say these words to remind himself that he was God's man. Then his mind would become calmer and clearer. Then he would be able to hear the counsel of the Holy Spirit guiding him to make the best decisions, strengthening him to fight off the tormenting temptations.

your picture of God

The picture of God which you carry in your mind is valuable. What you think he is like will have a lot to do with the way you think and speak and act. If he is really the Lord your God, if you really belong to him, then you will want to be like him no matter where you are or what you are doing.

What is God like? Many books have been written, apart from the Bible, describing God. The writers use all the best words they can find. They say that God is holy, perfect, good, kind, all-powerful, all-knowing, love itself. But the easiest way to see what God is like is to look at Jesus.

Maybe you have a hard time understanding this truth. Don't feel discouraged. One of Jesus' disciples, Philip, had a hard time understanding, too. Once when Philip was with Jesus in the Upper Room, he asked the Master if he and the other disciples could see God. "Show us the Father," said Philip, "and we shall be satisfied." Jesus answered him softly, "Have I been with you so long, and yet you do not know me, Philip? He who has seen me has seen the Father." (Read John 14:8-11.) Jesus wanted his disciples and everyone to know that he was God himself.

When men saw Jesus healing the rotting flesh of lepers or holding little children on his lap or telling the good news of the gospel to poor men and rich men alike, they saw the way God acted with his people. They saw the compassion on his face when he realized that a great crowd of people, five thousand in number, which had sat by the seaside listening to his teachings for three days, didn't have enough food. Right away Jesus wanted to care for their bodily needs. They saw the sadness in Jesus' eyes as he sat above the city of Jerusalem weeping because there were so many who refused to turn from their sinful ways. They saw the love in Jesus' face when he was nailed to that brutal cross. Even as the nails were driven into his hands, he prayed, "Father, forgive them; for they know not what they do."

This is the picture of God which Jesus would leave with you. This is your God, a God of tenderness and compassion and love. This is your Lord, who claims you as his own.

your sonship

Part of being God's son is to have a responsibility toward others. The way we conduct our lives will either bring other people closer to God or drive them further away from him. There is no doubt about what Jesus expects of us. As he said in the Sermon on the Mount, "Let your light so shine before men, that they may see your good works and give glory to your Father who is in heaven" (Matthew 5:16).

During the Middle Ages, a boy was born in the city of Carthage in North Africa. He was called Augustine. As he grew up, he wondered what he should do with his life. His home was divided; his father was a pagan and his mother was a Christian. For a long time Augustine felt that he should do whatever he wanted to do. So he spent most of his time with the wild, unruly pagan youth of his town. His mother was heartsick. But she never gave up trying to influence her son. She prayed for his change of heart; she tried to live a Christian life as an example to him. Finally the day came when Augustine came to his senses. He saw himself for what he really was—not a happy-go-lucky pagan who had no need of

God, but a man sick with disgust at his own meaningless life. Augustine became a Christian; his life now had value and purpose. He never forgot the influence of his mother, who played a large part in his decision. The light of her Christian personality radiated the truth about God.

Later in his life Augustine became a great leader of the church. He wrote a number of books about the importance of the Christian faith. One of the things he said was, "Love God and do as you please." This sounds like a strange statement to make. But Augustine knew what he was talking about. He had spent too many years doing just what he pleased without loving God. It didn't work. But when he came to love and trust God, then his life was turned inside out. Then he learned that when a person really loves God he wants to do that which pleases God. As God's son, therefore, you want the glory of the Father to shine through you because you love him. You no longer want indifference or lovelessness or willful disobedience to block God's will for your life.

As people who believe that the Lord is our God, we have a whole new attitude toward life. We get away from this business of always asking, "What do I want from life?" Instead we begin to ask, "What can I, as a son of God, give to life? How can I serve God and men?"

The Ten Commandments, as seen through Christ's eyes, are part of God's answer to those questions.

INTRODUCTION:

I AM THE LORD YOUR GOD

Part Two

Our Relationship with God

6

GOD COMES FIRST

Isaiah tells a story about a foolish little pagan who made himself a god. One day this man went out in the woods and cut down a tree. Half of the tree he chopped up into kindling wood. Then he built a fire with the wood, cooked his meat, baked his bread. Quite contentedly he sat in the warmth of the fire as he ate. "Aha," he said to himself, "I am warm, I have seen the fire!" Then he went to work on the other half of the tree, carving it into an idol. When he finished, he fell down before his homemade god and worshiped it. He even prayed to it. "Deliver me, for thou art my god!" he said reverently. (Read Isaiah 44:14-17.)

TO READ AND THINK ABOUT

Isaiah 44:14-17   How to Make a "god"
Matthew 6:24-33   Seeking God and Serving Him
Matthew 19:16-22   The Rich Young Ruler
Acts 17:22-31   Paul Speaks of the "Unknown God"
Ephesians 4:4-6   The One God
Isaiah 55:6-11   God's Ways Are Higher Than Man's
Psalm 19:1-6   "The Glory of God"

You may chuckle at the antics of Isaiah's happy-go-lucky pagan. How silly he was! Men should know better than to think they can make a god for themselves. But they keep on trying.

This was certainly true at the time when the people of Israel were traveling through the wilderness toward the land of promise. Every nation about them had, not one, but many man-made gods. Even though the Hebrews were slaves in Egypt, there was still danger that they might have accepted some of the attractive gods of their masters. God wanted to clear the air of any doubt or confusion. If he were to be the Lord their God, then they could have no other gods at all.

the gods of ignorance

When you study world history, you discover that every nation— in fact, every race of primitive people—has had some kind of god. Man has always sensed that the world didn't happen by accident. He has been aware of powers and forces he can't explain, so he has established a god or gods and worshiped them. It may be a sun god because the sun gives light and strength for plants to grow; it may be a rain god because water is essential to all forms of life. On the other hand, he may develop gods that have superhuman abilities. These gods look like men, but they are stronger and more powerful. They can hurl down thunderbolts from the sky or ride the hurricane. When people don't know the true God, their ignorance leads them to fashion gods of their own.

God chose the Hebrews as his people to set an example for the rest of the world. He let them know that he was the one God, the only God for all men. The Jews had a responsibility to share this amazing truth with others. It was only natural that the followers of Jesus, who was himself a Jew, felt the same responsibility. So the Christian church has always accepted the joyous task of missionary work. The church has a mission to tell all those who are ignorant of God about the heavenly Father who loved the world so much that he sent it his Son.

Paul, the greatest of all Christian missionaries, fought ignorance and superstition wherever he went. On one memorable day, he was invited to preach a sermon in Athens, Greece. Athens was a city of art and beauty. Statues to various gods and goddesses of Greek mythology were all about. Paul told the men who came to hear him speak that he thought they were very religious. He saw the gods that they worshiped all about him. He also found an altar with an inscription on it, "To an unknown god." It looked like the Greeks, with all the gods they had, still didn't want to risk missing a god they didn't know about. This "unknown" god, said Paul, was the God he wanted to tell them about. "The God who made the world and everything in it, being Lord of heaven and earth," Paul went on, "does not live in shrines made by man, nor is he served by human hands, as though he needed anything, since he himself gives to all men life and breath and everything." (Read Acts 17:22-31.)

the gods of choice

It is easy to understand the importance of the First Commandment to people who do not know about "God the Father Almighty, Maker of heaven and earth, and Jesus Christ his only Son our Lord." But of what importance is the commandment to those who do know about God? We certainly don't go around carving up trees to make gods of our own, or building altars to unknown gods. Yes, but it is still possible to have other gods in the place of the one and true God. Simply believing that God exists does not necessarily mean that you worship him and him alone.

Martin Luther said that a god is "that to which we look for all good and where we go for help in every time of need; to have a god is simply to trust and believe in one with our whole heart." In other words, we can make gods out of whatever we think are the most important things in life. We do this by our own free choice, too.

Some people want to make a god out of science, arguing that science offers man the good life through its new discoveries and inventions; that science, given enough time and laboratory space, can solve the world's problems. Other people would like to make a god of their country, feeling that their political leaders will always decide what is best for their citizens. Then there are people who prefer to have an economic system like communism or socialism as their god. As far as they are concerned, the system offers salvation. Sometimes, as in Russia and China, scientism, statism, and communism can get all mixed up together in the minds of many. One thing for sure, whatever a person puts in the place of the one and only God is a false god! Science and politics and economics are our servants, not our masters.

On the other hand, human beings have a number of desires and interests that can crowd God out. When this happens, their lives get dangerously out of balance. Sooner or later, they discover that the things they thought were more important than God are now actually controlling them.

For instance, one man may feel that money is the most important thing in life. Therefore, he spends most of his waking hours trying to get more money. Another man may want personal power and prestige more than anything else. He uses all his efforts to "get ahead," to climb to the top of the ladder in his business or profession so that he can make other people do what he wants them to. A woman can easily make her home all-important, spending all her energies to make it a showplace, the envy of her neighbors. Another woman may be totally concerned with herself and her appearance; her biggest concerns in life are the latest fashions and the cosmetics that will make her appearance even more attractive. Let's face it. A person can make God take a back seat in his life, or even ignore God altogether, by putting anything he wants in God's place— science, sex, his country, his job, even those he loves.

Are there "other gods" like these that you may be putting in place of God? Just because you are not completely grown up yet doesn't mean that you can't have the same gods adults do. On the other hand, you may have some special interests, such as your gang, your possessions, the sports you like, that become so important to you it is hard to keep God first. You can easily let a movie star or a sports hero take God's place if you want to. There are many ways that you can deny that God is important.

One thing is certain: you can't have any other god in your life and still have the one, true God. It is really quite simple. There can be only one center around which your life revolves.

Jesus pointed out clearly that no one can have two centers to his life simultaneously. He put it this way: "No one can serve two masters; for either he will hate the one and love the other, or he will be devoted to the one and despise the other. You cannot serve God and mammon" (Matthew 6:24).

The word "mammon" means a man's material wealth, his possessions. But mammon means possessions in a twisted way—when they become so important that they take the place of God. There is nothing wrong with saving money, having nice clothes, belonging to a good swim club, owning a new racing bike. The problem comes when things like these crowd God out of your life.

Some people think that Jesus loved the poor people and disliked the rich. That's not true. He loved the poor and the rich alike. Jesus never said that it was wrong to have money or other things of value. He simply wanted everyone to put first things first in their lives.

THE FIRST COMMANDMENT:
YOU SHALL HAVE NO OTHER GODS

That is why he said what he did to the rich young ruler who wanted to know what to do to have eternal life.

This young man was very wealthy; he had many prized possessions. He was a good man. He tried to live faithfully by the Ten Commandments. Jesus liked him very much, but he saw that the young ruler had a stumbling block in his life. "If you would be perfect," Jesus told him, "go, sell what you possess and give to the poor, and you will have treasure in heaven; and come, follow me." (Read Matthew 19:16-22.) The young man went away sorrowing. He just couldn't part with his possessions.

Jesus wasn't being mean. He knew that no man can have two gods to worship at the same time. Each one of us has to make a choice. To each of us Jesus says, "Go, get rid of whatever you have in the place of God . . . and come, follow me."

making idols

If you looked up the First Commandment in Exodus 20, you noticed that there was more to it than simply having no other gods. The commandment continues, "You shall not make yourself a graven image, or any likeness of anything that is in heaven above,

or that is in the earth beneath, or that is in the water under the earth; you shall not bow down to them or serve them . . ." (Exodus 20:4-5).

Some denominations make this the Second Commandment. But the Lutheran church and the Roman Catholic church have always considered these verses part of the First Commandment.

The numbering really makes little difference. The point is that, along with having "no other gods," God wants us to know that he cannot be imprisoned in a statue. A "graven image" is an idol, some man-made object used for worship. The main trouble with idols is that some misguided persons might think that God actually lives in this little carved piece of wood or glass or stone.

The Jews took this commandment so seriously that they never developed any of the arts like painting or sculpture. That is why, incidentally, no pictures of Jesus or his disciples were ever painted from life. But this part of the First Commandment doesn't really forbid art; it forbids trying to capture God in one spot. There is nothing wrong with having a painting of Christ on the walls of your room or a statue of Christ in your church. But if you pray to him as though he were in that painting or sculpture, you are reducing him to an idol. He is too great to be limited by any man-made objects, no matter how beautiful those objects are.

magic

Another problem with idols is that worship gets turned into magic. Some people drive around with little statues of saints fastened to the cowl of their dashboards; many believe that these figurines will protect them from harm on the road. This is not much different from those soldiers who carry a copy of the Bible in their shirt pockets over their hearts. The power of God's Word just might stop a bullet.

Magic is trying to get God to do what you want him to do. Worship, on the other hand, is giving yourself to God with praise for what he has done for you. No wonder Moses got so angry with the people when they made a golden calf and worshiped it. He had just come down from Mount Sinai with the Ten Commandments under his arm and here were his people trying to tell God what to do. Moses dramatically smashed the stones of the Commandments to bits to bring the Hebrews to their senses.

We do not have a god to use as we see fit; we have a God who gives us his blessings and uses us to share his blessings with others.

the meaning of the first commandment

What does the First Commandment mean? Luther answered that question with eleven words, "We are to fear, love, and trust God above anything else." This means simply putting God first in your life.

Let's look at the verbs Luther uses. Each one is important.

To Fear God. This doesn't mean to be afraid of God. It means to honor him so much that you want to do whatever pleases him. This kind of fear is associated with words like awe and respect. If you hold someone in high regard, you have no desire to do anything that would hurt him or make him ashamed of you. You might even say, "I'd be afraid to do anything that would make him sad." This is the kind of fear we should have toward God "above anything else."

To Love God. Love is the outpouring of yourself. When you truly love someone, you give all that you have and are to him. Nothing is held back. To love God above anything else is to give your complete loyalty and devotion to him. In any decision that you have to make, in any problem that you have to solve, you put your relationship to God first.

To Trust God. Trust is confidence. To trust God above anything else is to believe that his promises are true, that he will never let you down. You know that he will always give you the strength to withstand temptation. You know that he will always give you the courage to bear whatever troubles and tragedies life brings. You know that his will for you is good, so you pray, "Thy will be done," without worrying about the future.

Keeping the First Commandment is not easy. We live in a world of many gods asking us to accept them. Every time we try to put something else in the place of God, the commandment judges us and exposes our willingness to find substitutes for him. Maybe when we are tempted to worship "other gods," it would be a good idea to repeat Paul's triumphant words: "There is . . . one Lord, one faith, one baptism, one God and Father of us all, who is above all and through all and in all" (Ephesians 4:4-6).

7

GOD'S NAME IS HOLY

When you were baptized, God gave his name to you. You are now a "child of God." He expects you to bear that name with pride. If you truly love God, you will not want to do anything to bring dishonor on his name. On the contrary, you will want your whole life, including your words and your thoughts, to express his holiness. To do any less than this is to misuse God's name. That is why the Second Commandment reminds you of your duty.

TO READ AND THINK ABOUT

Exodus 3:13-17   God Gives His Name to Moses
Psalm 99:1-5   Praise God's Name
Micah 4:1-5   Walk in the Name of God
Luke 1:46-55   Mary's Song
John 17:6-19   Jesus Makes God's Name Meaningful
Matthew 5:33-37   Don't Swear at All
Romans 10:9-13   Riches of God's Name

Many people think the Second Commandment refers only to the way we use God's name when we speak. They seem to have a mental picture of God as a cranky old gentleman who is fussy about anyone using his name for any purpose other than prayer or praise. They feel that this commandment was given to stop any habit we might have of salting our conversations with petty profanity.

The use of vile language is very common today. Some people use "dirty words," vulgar expressions, and even the name of God to show that they are big and tough. Others may use these words out of sheer ignorance if they hear them repeated in their presence often enough. Sometimes it seems that almost everywhere you turn you hear or see words that remind you of filth and ugliness. Many books, plays, and films use these words for their shocking effect. We need the Second Commandment to remind us that our speaking should be holy. The words we choose to speak and the way we speak them is one more way to let other people know that we belong to God.

But the Second Commandment is much bigger and more important to our relationship with God than simply controlling our language. It confronts us with the challenge that, if we accept God as our Lord, we must live as his sons. If we call ourselves Christians, then we are obligated to think and speak and work and play as disciples of Christ. Otherwise we take the name of God upon our lives "in vain."

your name

Think for a moment about your own name. It's important to you, isn't it? Your name stands for you.

Most people are proud of their names. They like to see their names in print; they like to hear their names spoken properly by others. Why? Simply because their names set them apart from everyone else.

Your name makes you an individual. Your name tells the world that you are not a member or a thing; you are a real person. Your name is really one of your most personal and private possessions.

Therefore, you want to keep your name honorable. You don't want anyone to tell lies about you that would damage your reputation. Nor do you want to have your name linked with actions that would make people think less of you. You want your name to stand for something good and fine and decent.

William Shakespeare spoke for most of us when he wrote:
Who steals my purse steals trash. . . .
But he that filches from me my good name
Robs me of that which not enriches him,
And makes me poor indeed.

The writer of Proverbs put it this way, "A good name is to be chosen rather than great riches, and favor is better than silver or gold" (Proverbs 22:1). You want your name to reflect your real worth and dignity—always. Your name is actually a symbol of the real you. When people see your name, they think of the living, real person that the name stands for.

the name of God

God's name is a symbol, too. When we use his name, the idea of what he is like flashes through our minds. He is not the sun or the rain or the stars that primitive people have worshiped as gods. He is the God who made us, the God who loves us, the God who gave us his Son Jesus Christ to be our Lord and Savior.

When God came to the Hebrew people, he told them who he was. As a matter of fact, Moses asked God point-blank what his name was. Said Moses, "If I come to the people of Israel and say to them, 'The God of your fathers has sent me to you,' and they ask me, 'What is his name?' what shall I say to them?" God said to Moses, "I AM WHO I AM. Say this to the people of Israel, 'I AM has sent me to you' " (Exodus 3:13-14).

YOU SHALL NOT TAKE THE NAME OF THE LORD YOUR GOD IN VAIN

"I AM"—that sounds like a strange name for God. But it did not seem strange to the Hebrews. It meant that God existed, that he always had been and always would be active in his world on their behalf because he had made them. Yet the Hebrews never used this name of God, even in their prayers; they felt it was too holy to be expressed by the sinful lips of men. So, in speaking of God, they often called him the Lord (or Father, as Jesus later taught them to do).

God's name is holy as God himself is holy. The Hebrews, as the people of God, were expected to live up to this name. Wherever they went, whatever they did, they were to call attention to the God whom they worshiped. If they did not, they were taking God's name "in vain." To take his name "in vain" means to empty it of its power and its meaningfulness, to make it seem unimportant. We also, like the Hebrew people, are expected to live up to God's name. And we also take God's name in vain every time we act as if we were not children of God at all.

Of course, you are using God's name in vain when you speak it idly as an exclamation or use it in connection with vulgar language, too. In using it casually or thoughtlessly, you are making it seem

unimportant. (Incidentally, words like "golly," "gosh," and "gee" are substitute words people dreamed up to use instead of the name of God.)

luther's explanation

The Second Commandment means, says Luther, "We are to fear and love God so that we do not use his name to curse, swear, lie, or deceive, but call on him in prayer, praise, and thanksgiving."

Luther wants us to realize that the whole reason for obeying this commandment is because we love God. We stand in awe before his greatness. We accept him as our God. Since we feel this way, it obviously follows that we want his glory to shine through us. We certainly use God's name wisely and appropriately when we pray to him or sing his praises or give him thanks for his many blessings. In this way, we open up our lives for God to come into our hearts. We allow him to shape us and make our personalities more like his. When we use phrases like "Thy kingdom come, thy will be done," we are asking God to be God, to carry out his plans for us. We are not worried about what he will do. We know how much he loves us.

43

Because God means so much to us, there are certain things we do not want to do with his name. Luther points out four evil uses to which people sometimes put God's name: cursing, swearing, lying, and deceiving.

cursing

Originally, a curse was a kind of prayer for harm or injury to someone. Since the Hebrews believed that words were living things, a curse once spoken could not be taken back. A curse wished the worst to happen. To say "God damn you" is to pray that God condemn a person to everlasting hell.

This is a terrible misuse of God's name even though many people curse without thinking about what they are saying. Carelessness is no real excuse. No man has the right to sit in judgment of another person and decide that person is worthless. Judgment is God's job. Neither has any man the power to tell God what to do. God will do what is just and loving no matter what we say. As his sons, our responsibility is to bless instead of curse, to forgive instead of bearing grudges, to wish the best things to happen instead of the worst.

swearing

There are two ways in which to understand the word "swearing."

Swearing is related to cursing in that it, too, can appeal to God to support a sinful human action. "By God, I'll kill you," says an angry man to his enemy. But where does the loving God really come into the picture? Does God want this killing to take place? Hardly!

On the other hand, swearing also can be an appeal to God in the form of a solemn oath to support truth that is being said. Most public officials take a solemn oath when they enter office to fulfill their duties "by the help of God." This is a respectful use of God's name and a conscious asking for his assistance.

Courts of law usually ask witnesses to swear that they will "tell the truth, the whole truth, and nothing but the truth, so help me God." Again this is a respectful use of God's name if the witness intends to give an honest and truthful testimony relying on God to help him do his best.

But the swearing in the first sense can easily become a careless, unthinking habit just as cursing can. Don't let it happen. For then you cheapen God's name as well as conduct yourself in a way that gives no glory to him.

lying, deceiving

God's name can be used in vain whenever someone appeals to God to twist the truth. In wartime, it is easy to think that God loves one country and not another. This is ridiculous. God loves all men even though he might not like what some of them are doing.

God's name has been used to support racial prejudice as though he loved people with one color of skin more than others. There are even those who think that God loves members of one religious denomination more than he does those of another. Can you think of other ways that God's name is used to support errors?

Sometimes we go through all the motions of being dedicated Christians in order to impress people, but secretly we do many unchristian things. Isn't this lying about our relationship to God? Aren't we deceiving others? You may display the Bible in a prominent place in your room and really never open it. Are you trying to make someone think that God means more to you than he really does? This, too, is taking God's name in vain.

God wants us to be honest, to be people he can trust. He doesn't want us to need to deceive anyone about our religious devotion. He wants us to be open and forthright about the fact that he is our God and that we belong to him. He wants us to bear his name with honor and pride.

"take good care of our name"

Have you ever read any of the fascinating short stories written by O. Henry? He was a fine author who always ended his tales with a delightful and unexpected twist. O. Henry's real name was William Sydney Porter. When Porter was a young man he was imprisoned in Texas for embezzling money. He became very friendly in jail with one of his guards, Oren Henry. He also started to write. When the time came to leave the prison, Porter decided to start life afresh and publish his stories under the pseudonym of "O. Henry," the name of his friend. As Porter walked through the prison gates a free man, the guard is supposed to have waved to him and said, "Take good care of our name."

8

HONORING THE WORD OF GOD

We live in a holiday-minded culture. This is probably true because we have more leisure time than ever before. Your great-grandfather probably worked six full days a week from sunup to sundown. Your grandfather did his work in five and a half days; your father may work only eight hours a day for five days a week. By the time you are ready to choose your life occupation, you may be only required to give four days a week to your job. But what will you do with the rest of your time?

TO READ AND THINK ABOUT

Exodus 20:9-11   Details of the Third Commandment
Isaiah 58:13-14   Honor the Day; Honor God
Ezekiel 20:10-20   The Meaning of the Sabbath
Mark 2:23-28   The Sabbath Made for Man
Luke 13:10-17   Jesus Heals on the Sabbath
Mark 3:1-6   Another Healing Miracle
Acts 20:7-12   Sleeping During a Sermon

Time comes from God. The God who made us and calls us his children put us in a world of distinct rhythm. Day follows night; spring follows winter. All of life has its rhythms, too—time to eat, time to sleep, time to work, and time to play. Our health and happiness depend upon developing good habits of living according to these rhythms. God knows what we need, so in his plan for the world he asks us to set aside a certain time, one day in every seven, as a special day of worship and rest. This special day is not only a holiday; it is a holy day. This is God's day, the day when his people especially remember their relationship with him.

But what can you do on a holy day? What can't you do? You probably have a lot of questions about the way a Christian acts on Sunday. Most people do. They tend to ask about their behavior patterns as though anything goes the rest of the week, but on Sunday they have to be different. "Can I play ball?" "Is it OK to cut the grass?" "How about Sunday movies?" "What about taking a long weekend trip with my family to the mountains or the seashore?" "If I go to church, can I have the rest of the day for myself?"

Answers to questions like these are not easy. There are no final answers. Each of us has to decide for himself what the Third Commandment means to him, not only in terms of how he spends the day the Lord has set aside, but also in terms of how he conducts himself on the other days of the week. Before we go any further with these problems, though, let's look carefully at Luther's understanding of this commandment from a Christian point of view.

sunday means worship

In his explanation of the Third Commandment, Luther has nothing to say about the Sabbath at all, as a day of rest or as any other kind of day. As far as he was concerned, "keeping the Sabbath" meant one thing—worship. Since people did not have to work, they could gather together as a congregation and praise God. They could listen to God's Word being read and preached; they could study their Bibles. Luther comes right to the point, "We are to fear and love God so that we do not neglect his Word and the preaching of it, but regard it as holy and gladly hear and learn it."

Notice that here, as always, Luther stresses our love of God. If we really love God, we are glad to be in his presence with our fellow Christians. We want to know what his Word has to say to us. This is the most important thing in life. A Christian, therefore, goes to his church services regularly not because he *has to* but because he *wants to*. There is no place he would rather be on Sunday than in the house of the Lord.

Along with worship, Luther underscores our need to study God's Word. On another occasion, Luther said, "The Word of God is the true holy thing above all holy things." Simply hearing the words of Scripture, then, isn't enough. We need time to study what these words mean for our lives. Christian education has always been one of the great ministries of the church.

One of the milk companies has the slogan "You never outgrow your need for milk." Luther could easily paraphrase that slogan, "You never outgrow your need for hearing and studying the Word of God." However, he did put it this way, "We Christians should make every day a holy day and give ourselves only to holy activities —that is, occupy ourselves daily with God's Word." Each month, each year, you grow and change. You are having new experiences. Your mind is expanding with new ideas. You constantly need to be exploring God's truth to see how your life may reflect his holiness.

the light in the darkness

There was a terrible time in world history called the Dark Ages. All over Europe wild tribes from the mountains and plains swept across the cities and towns, burning, ravaging, destroying. Civilization seemed on the brink of slipping back into barbarism. But the

REMEMBER THE SABBATH DAY TO KEEP IT HOLY

Christian church kept the light of truth burning. Little churches here and there kept their days of worship and rallied people around their faith in God. The churches taught God's Word and taught men to read and preach it. So strong did the church finally become that many of the wild barbarian hordes were converted to Christianity.

Our world today is really not much different from the world of the Dark Ages. We are in constant danger. Cold wars and hot wars are still going on. Worldliness and selfishness threaten to destroy truth. Christianity is always one generation away from dying out. But the light of truth is in our hands. We are the heirs of the disciples. It is our task to join them in keeping the faith burning brightly. Only with regular, joyful worship of God, only with constant, intelligent study of his Word, are we equipped to carry on Christ's work through his church. Obviously, this means not only using Sunday for these purposes but also making every day an opportunity to draw close to God.

Because the Christian sees much more in the Third Commandment than did the Jew, we need to examine it closely. Perhaps we will find some clues to explain why so many people get sidetracked into thinking that keeping the commandment is a simple matter of correct behavior on one certain day of the week.

the jewish sabbath

The Hebrew word "sabbath" means to break off or cease. In other words, the Jew was to stop whatever he had been doing on other days of the week to do something else on the Sabbath. When Moses gave the Commandments to the Hebrews, he reported exactly what God said about this "doing something else."

Six days you shall labor, and do all your work; but the seventh day is a sabbath to the LORD your God; in it you shall not do any work, you, or your son, or your daughter, your manservant, or your maidservant, or your cattle, or the sojourner who is within your gates; for in six days the Lord made heaven and earth, the sea, and all that is in them, and rested the seventh day; therefore the LORD blessed the sabbath day and hallowed it (Exodus 20:9-11).

Even apart from the religious significance of the Sabbath, God knew that living things must have regular periods of rest. This was true not only for human beings but for animals as well. Therefore, there had to be an appointed time for work to stop.

Most nations recognize the necessity of a weekday of rest. Some countries have had to pass laws to prevent greedy bosses from working their employees beyond their endurance. Interestingly enough,

49

Communist Russia, a country that officially denies the very existence of God, still insists on the weekly rest day.

The ancient Jews were very strict about Sabbath observance. They drew up hundreds of rules and regulations saying what a Jew could and could not do on the Sabbath. Anyone who broke the Sabbath rules was punished. Gradually, however, they made the Sabbath a burden instead of a blessing. There is even a case on record of a Jew being stoned to death because he had gathered firewood on the Sabbath.

Jesus and the sabbath

By the time Jesus lived, the Sabbath laws had become a legalistic straitjacket. And Jesus himself got in trouble with the Jewish authorities several times.

On one occasion, as he and his disciples were walking through some grainfields, the disciples picked the ears of ripened grain. Rubbing the ears in their fingers, they separated the grain kernels and ate them. Since this happened to be the Sabbath, some Pharisees who saw the incident complained to Jesus, "Look, why are they doing what is not lawful on the sabbath?" You see, the disciples, in rubbing the ears of grain, were winnowing the grain. This was "work." Not only that, but they picked the grain off the stalks— "reaping," more "work." It sounds like a ridiculous charge. But the Pharisees, the watchdogs of the Jewish laws, were deadly serious about it.

Jesus answered them with an unforgettable remark: "The sabbath was made for man, not man for the sabbath; so the Son of man is lord even of the sabbath." (Read the whole account of this incident in Mark 2:23-28.) Jesus was saying that human needs, such as the hunger of his disciples, have to be met. A loving God certainly wants to care for his people even on this special day. Jesus called himself the Son of man and pointed out that he—certainly not the Pharisees—was lord over the Sabbath.

Another time Jesus went into a synagogue on the Sabbath and chanced to meet there a man whose hand was twisted and deformed. There were some Pharisees there who watched carefully to see what Jesus would do. If he healed on this day, he would be breaking the law and they could accuse him. Jesus suddenly asked the religious leaders a tricky question. "Is it lawful on the sabbath to do good or to do harm, to save life or to kill?" No one answered. So Jesus healed the withered hand of the man who suffered. (See Mark 3:1-6.) Doing good was simply doing the will of God as far as Jesus was concerned. There never is a day when God would not want his people to heal and help one another. It is not what you don't do on the Sabbath, but what you do, that counts.

The seventh day of the week was Saturday. So the Jews have generally kept Saturday as the Sabbath. From sundown on Friday evening to sundown on Saturday evening was God's holy day. Some modern groups like the Seventh-Day Adventists agree with the Jews and use Saturday for worship. The followers of Christ, however, have accepted Sunday as the special day to glorify God.

Now there is no command in the Bible that we should keep Sunday holy. The Christians did so because Jesus rose from the dead on Easter, which was the first day of a new week. Every Sunday (remember the name of this day is pagan—it is named for the sun) the Christians celebrated Easter. Their Lord lived! As he rose from the dead, so they, too, would one day join in the resurrection and be united with him forever. This was something to be joyful about. Then, too, the Christian church was born on a Sunday, on Pentecost. God did not leave his people helpless when Jesus had gone from their sight. He sent the Holy Spirit to forge them into the living fellowship of the church. Here was another good reason for the early Christian to emphasize Sunday as a special day to glorify God.

For a long time the Christians continued to gather to worship God on the seventh day of the week. But they also got together faithfully after work or early in the morning on Sunday. Then they expressed their thanks to God for his great gifts of forgiveness of sins and life everlasting. It wasn't until the fourth century that Constantine the Great, emperor of the Roman Empire, made Sunday a legal holiday and therefore a legal holy day for the Christians. No more did they have to work on the first day of the week. They could devote their time to glorifying God.

the Lord's day

There are some people who would like to change the name of Sunday to the Lord's Day. This, they argue, would be a good thing. It would, by its very name, remind people what they owe to God. However, there is danger in this suggestion—we might forget that every day is the Lord's Day.

Keeping the Lord's Day holy isn't a matter of some things being right to do and some things being wrong. It isn't a matter of right or wrong at all; it is a matter of what is appropriate. What we do on Sunday should be done to give special honor to God. As we rest from the workday week, we spend some time in the presence of our heavenly Father. This is a time to measure our lives against the perfect life of his Son Jesus. This is a time to listen intently to God's Word as it is read from the Bible and preached and made meaningful through the sacraments. And what is more important, to rejoice in the privilege of worshiping. The Lord's Day—Sunday—is a happy day.

Suppose you had a birthday party and invited your friends. When they came, however, they hardly noticed that you were around. They spent their time having fun, giving presents to one another and doing whatever pleased them. You would feel pretty sad. You would feel that their actions were inappropriate. This was your day, and your friends were supposed to be paying special attention to you.

But this is the way we often treat God. Especially at Christmas, on the birthday of his Son! This is the way we can disobey the Third Commandment—by turning Sunday into a selfish day. Whenever we choose our own selfish interests first and put God in second place, we have lost the holiness and true value of the Sabbath. Here is a clue to your questions about what should or should not be done on Sunday.

Playing games is rest and relaxation for many people. But should they selfishly insist that other people work on Sunday in order to provide them with entertainment? Putting God first in our thinking suggests that we should help other people put God first on this holy day, too.

the first three commandments

Look back for a moment over the first three commandments. All of them have to do with our relationship to God. Some people speak of these three as "The First Table of the Law." Here God tells us that he expects us to put him first in our lives. He also wants us to carry his name with pride and honor. Further, he expects us to revere his Word, to hear and learn it gladly at all times. And, in order to do this, he expects us to observe regular periods of worship and prayer, particularly on the Lord's Day.

There are seven other commandments that God has given us telling us how we are to live with our fellowmen. But these seven commandments have no real meaning unless we accept and obey the first three.

52

Part Three

Our Relationship with Others

9

YOU AND YOUR FAMILY

"No man is an island." So wrote the great poet John Donne. You don't need to be a brilliant thinker like Donne to realize the truth of his remark. You know that as an individual you are never alone. You belong to a human family. As a matter of fact, this happened without your approval. You had no choice of parents. You were born into a world with close human ties that will always be part of you. Getting along with your parents is one of your very important responsibilities not only as a human being but as a Christian.

TO READ AND THINK ABOUT

Ephesians 6:1-3   Obey and Honor
Colossians 3:18-25   Christian Family Living
Proverbs 1:8-9; 19:26-27   Good Advice
1 Timothy 5:1-8   Taking Care of Family
John 19:26-27   Jesus and His Mother
Romans 13:1-7   Respect for Authority
1 Peter 2:13-17   Living Under Authority

God must have thought that the kind of life we live in our family circles is very important. He gave the commandment about our relationship to our parents immediately after he had described the ways in which we are to honor him. In a sense, the Fourth Commandment is a bridge between our duties to God and our duties to our fellowmen. Parents are God's representatives. They are the ones who first give us an understanding of who God is. They also teach us our first lessons in the ways we must act toward others.

God's gift of parents

In God's plan for his world, he decided that the human family would be the building block of civilization. The family is a magnificent way of insuring that human life will flow on from generation to generation, preserving cultural values and developing responsibility in the individual. For this reason God created both man and woman. Out of their life together would come new life, a child. Out of the parents' love for each other would come a love for this child and a desire to help him grow and develop as a child of God.

Sometimes you may wish that you did not have to be so dependent on your parents. You would like to grow up in a hurry so that you could do what you want to do. But growing up takes time. You have to learn to crawl before you can walk; you have to walk before you can run.

In one of L. Frank Baum's "Wizard of Oz" stories, he described a peculiar kind of people called the Mangaboos. The Mangaboos, who lived in the center of the earth, grew on vines like vegetables. When they grew to be adults they were considered "ripe" and were picked from the vines. But by then their lives were almost half over. There are few people who would really prefer trading slow flesh-and-blood living for rapid Mangaboo living. Imagine being picked from a vine at the ripe old age of, let's say, twenty-one and finding yourself alive in a strange and wonderful world. Think of the questions you would have. "Who am I?" "Where am I?" "What do I do with this life that I have?"

God has planned it so that, from your earliest days, you know that you are a person to be loved. You have a personality all your own; your family lets you know that they are happy to have you join them. Your father and your mother have given you part of themselves. You belong to them through strong physical ties. But as you grow older, they help you understand that you also belong to God. Thus, they help you grow up to be the kind of person who not only knows he is loved and respected for himself, but who also knows how to love. The true test of maturity is the ability to love both God and your fellowmen. Remember, Jesus summarized all the Commandments by saying that we have the responsibility to love God and to love our neighbors as ourselves.

Since the family is so vital in God's scheme of life, he gave us two commandments dealing with family life. One is directed toward preserving the intimacy of marriage between one man and one woman—the Sixth Commandment. The other, the Fourth Commandment, asks each person to honor and respect his parents, who have brought him into the world and have contributed so much to his taking his place in the world.

the "gimme" way of life

When you were young, you probably wrote long letters to Santa Claus. You told him all the things you wanted for Christmas. Usually you asked for a lot more toys and gifts than you really needed or wanted. You were hoping to get some of the things that were dear to your heart. Maybe Christmas for you was in terms of "gimme this" or "gimme that." Maybe it still is.

A lot of people have a "gimme" way of life. You can understand this attitude in a child. But when the child becomes a youth, he needs to realize the joy of giving to others. Paul stressed this idea when he quoted Jesus' teachings: "It is more blessed to give than to receive" (Acts 20:35).

Some people think of their parents only in "gimme" terms. They are only interested in what they can get from their mothers and fathers. Far from being thankful for what they do receive, they are always demanding more. Sometimes when they don't get what they want, they turn against their parents in anger and hatred.

When John F. Kennedy became President, he said to all citizens in his Inaugural Address, "Ask not what your country can do for you, ask what you can do for your country." Perhaps, in the Fourth Commandment, God is saying, "Ask not what your parents can do for you, ask what you can do for them."

honor and other verbs

As Luther tried to explain the meaning of the Fourth Commandment in simple terms, he found himself adding verbs. Besides honoring our parents, we should "respect, obey, love, and serve them," said Luther. He wanted us to understand what honor means.

In view of Luther's family background, this may seem rather surprising. Luther had a very unhappy boyhood at times. His father, Hans, was a miner who seldom understood his son. Luther often found himself in disagreement with both his mother and father. When he decided to leave law school and enter the priesthood, his parents objected. They wanted Martin to be an influential lawyer, a man of position and property; they didn't want him lost behind monastery walls. Yet, despite his difficulties, Luther loved and honored his parents.

From his own experiences, he knew that there are times when parents and children don't understand each other or get angry with each other. However, none of our problems can be so severe that we have a right to turn against our parents, to hurt them, or to ignore them. As Christians, we honor them because of their place in God's plan for our lives. Without them we wouldn't have life. Further, as Christians, we need to help them when they need our aid. We should respect them and love them for all that they are and have done for us.

How about obedience? We can go along with Luther as long as

THE FOURTH COMMANDMENT:

HONOR YOUR FATHER AND YOUR MOTHER

he uses sweet and noble words like honor, love, and respect. What about the harsh word obey? That is a little harder. Yet here is the key to our real relationships with our parents. They have had wider experience of life; they have already wrestled with most of the problems that we are just now meeting. Their discipline of us is born of their love for us. Why does your dad go over and over the safety rules when you use the power mower? He knows the dangers of carelessness in handling a rapidly moving blade. Why does your mother keep insisting that you wash your hands and face before a meal? She knows that dirt breeds germs and germs can make you sick. It sounds so simple. But sometimes the hardest lesson we have to learn is that our parents may know more than we do.

Mark Twain, the humorous author of *Tom Sawyer*, was talking with several friends about the problems of growing up. "You know," he said, "when I was sixteen I thought my father was ignorant. But when I became twenty-one I was amazed to discover how much my father had learned in the last five years."

parents aren't perfect

Of course, your parents aren't perfect; neither are you. We all need the forgiving love of God. And as we pray for God's forgiveness, we are reminded, too, of our responsibility to forgive one another daily.

Don't bother to count up the times you have needed to ask your parents' forgiveness for things you did that were wrong. It would be a long list, wouldn't it? And how about the many times they have forgiven you when you didn't have the courage to ask them to? Well, there are times when you need to forgive your parents if they have wronged you. This is the power of love; it can heal hurts and overlook differences.

You see, the point is not whether you think your parents are worthy of your love and respect. You count them as worthy because God has selected them to be your earthly family. You have a responsibility to honor them and to care for them always.

Jesus gave us the most striking example of how a son honors his mother. Even though Mary misunderstood his ministry at times, still she was there at the foot of the cross when Jesus died. Hanging on the cruel wooden crossbeam, he looked down in agony and saw his mother standing by his disciple John. Even though the pain was searing, Jesus thought of her future. He wanted to be sure that she would be cared for.

Slowly he spoke. He told Mary that she was now to think of John as her son. And John was to take Mary into his home and look after her just as though she were his own mother. (Read John 19:26-27.) In honoring Mary, whom God himself chose to be Jesus' mother, Jesus was giving honor to God.

"We are to fear and love God so that we do not despise or anger our parents and others in authority, but respect, obey, and love, and serve them." This is Luther's whole reason for obedience to the Fourth Commandment.

Because we love God, because we stand in awe of his magnificent plan for life on the earth, we honor those whom he has chosen to be responsible for us.

Paul wrote some advice to the tiny mission congregation in Ephesus telling the Christians there what was expected of them. To these people, living on the coast of what is now Turkey, he said, "Children, obey your parents in the Lord, for this is right. 'Honor your father and mother' (this is the first commandment with a promise), 'that it may be well with you and that you may live long on the earth' " (Ephesians 6:1-3).

Note Paul's phrase "parents in the Lord." This is the point that Luther wants us to understand. Note also that, when Paul quotes the commandment, he mentions the promise connected with it. If you read the account of the giving of the Ten Commandments, you saw the promise there—"that your days may be long in the land which the LORD your God gives you" (Exodus 20:12). Does this mean that we accept God's gift of our parents in order to guarantee a long life for ourselves? That would seem selfish.

Actually, what this promise means is that we will have lasting satisfaction and contentment. To have a happy home life, to enjoy the presence of your family, is to share in God's richest blessings. When we obey his will for us in the way we live with our parents, we are really accepting the nature of life itself. God gave parents authority; we are to respect it. "Honor your father and your mother," Luther once wrote. "It is the grandest work we can do next to the sublime task of worshiping God."

other authority

Let's carry this idea of authority a step further. When Luther describes our duties to our parents, he adds that we have the same duties to "others in authority."

The home is really the world in miniature. Here is teaching and worship and government. But many families find that they can do many more things for the good of their children if they pool their talents and interests with other families in the community. So they build schools and hire teachers; they erect their churches and call pastors to serve them. They elect representatives from among them to set up a form of government. To all these people whom families give authority—the teacher, the pastor, the governor—Luther says we should give honor and respect.

Our kind of free, democratic society can be effective only if we support the people whom we have given authority. If you misbehave in your classes at school and show disrespect for your teachers, they have to spend their valuable time disciplining you. The loss of this time robs both you and others in your class of education. Think how much money could be spent on parks and highways and public buildings if it didn't cost our city and state governments so much to fight crime. The person who refuses to respect authority helps break down the orderliness of God's world. He also spoils the happiness and contentment of a satisfying life, both for himself and others.

As sinful people who like to go on their own way, we need authority over us to remind us of our duties and responsibilities. According to God's plan, then, we are to obey the authorities whether we want to or not. Of course, God expects those in authority to be fair and just. The only time Christians are justified in disobedience is when authority runs counter to the Word of God. When this happens, we must remember that God comes first; we must always obey God rather than men.

Our task as citizens and as Christians is to learn to discipline ourselves. This has to happen first in the family circle and then in the ever-widening circles of life outside the home. Even though we might not like the person who is our teacher or pastor, even though we might disagree with the person elected to public office, we need to honor and obey them. In doing so, we give honor to God, who made possible the office of authority which they hold. This is the only way that society can be orderly and dependable. This is the only way that we can work for an ever-better community and world in which to live.

RESPECT FOR HUMAN LIFE

Sometimes it takes a disaster to remind people that all men are brothers. In the summer of 1962, great earthquakes rocked the mountain areas of Iran. Thousands of people were killed; countless thousands of others were injured and left homeless. Immediately, many nations rushed rescue teams to the devastated area. Planes landed at Iran's airports, one right after another, bringing cargoes of food, clothing, medicine. It was not an unusual sight to see a Negro Red Cross worker assisting an Oriental doctor as he gave blood plasma to a white child. A Communist might be working alongside a capitalist to rescue people trapped beneath the rubble of a collapsed building. Christians and Jews often found themselves setting up rude field hospitals together to care for Moslems. All that mattered was that here were human beings in desperate need; somebody had to help them.

TO READ AND THINK ABOUT

Luke 10:25-37   The Good Samaritan
Matthew 5:21-22   Jesus' Teachings on Anger
Matthew 5:38-45   Love Your Enemies
Luke 23:33-34   Jesus' Example
1 John 3:11-18   Hate Is Murder
Romans 12:14-21   Overcoming Evil
1 Corinthians 6:19-20   Glorify God with Your Body

This kind of human action—caring for the needs of others—was dear to the heart of Jesus. The whole purpose of his Parable of the Good Samaritan was to describe what it means to be neighborly. Being neighborly is helping anyone in need. In contrast with the robbers who beat the merchant unmercifully and cared nothing for his life, stands the nameless Samaritan who felt that human life was important. Jesus taught that life is the gift of God to all men. Therefore, all men have an obligation to protect and preserve life.

human life is sacred

God's point of view is clearly expressed in the Ten Commandments. Immediately after his commandment concerning the way we are to live with our families and those in authority, he reminds us in the Fifth Commandment that we are united with all other human beings by the gift of life. Only God has the privilege of determining when life begins and when it should end.

Two bums in New York City wandered by mistake into a crowd gathered around a street-corner evangelist. He was standing on a crate preaching about the Ten Commandments. When the sermon was over, one bum said to the other, "Well, at least I never killed anybody." The Fifth Commandment is one of the most-obeyed. Practically every nation and every religion agree that it is wrong to murder. Most people feel that the worst sin they can commit is the act of killing another person.

the real sin behind murder

Maybe you feel that since you and your classmates are all Christians, you don't need to spend much time talking about killing. You aren't planning to go out and murder someone. But can all of you control your tempers and prevent anger or hatred from leading you to do terrible things? It may be that no one is as innocent of breaking this commandment as he may think he is.

Of course, the person who willfully takes the life of another because of anger, or disagreement, or hope of gain, or any of a hundred reasons is going directly against God's holy will. This is murder in the first degree, to use a legal term. A murderer has decided on his own that another person must die. This is a decision no man has the right to make.

The thought is father of the deed. Behind every act of deliberate murder is the opinion that someone should die. Jesus, knowing the way people can get all twisted up in their thinking, had some significant things to say about the Fifth Commandment in the Sermon on the Mount (Matthew 5:21-22). Let's look very carefully at what he had to say.

"You have heard that it was said to the men of old, 'You shall not kill; and whoever kills shall be liable to judgment.' "

Jesus was talking to the Jews; he was reminding them of their Jewish traditions. The Jewish law provided severe penalties for killing. ("Whoever strikes a man so that he dies shall be put to death," Exodus 21:12.)

"But I say to you that every one who is angry with his brother shall be liable to judgment. . . ."

Jesus was not changing the commandment; he was giving it a far deeper meaning by pointing out the relationship of anger to killing. You've heard the phrase "If looks could kill." It is possible to kill a person mentally. The only thing that keeps some people from actually killing is fear of punishment. What these people do not realize is that God, who judges our actions, judges the motivations of our hearts as well. "Brother" means every man, in Jesus' thinking.

". . . Whoever insults his brother shall be liable to the council. . . ."

To insult a person is to show contempt for him. This shows contempt for God's creation. Whenever you look down on another person with a sneer, as though he were inferior to you, you are again ignoring God's will that we accept all people as he does. In love, God created human life and planned for every person to love him forever. Another person may not have your skin color or your intelligence or your athletic ability or your beauty, but he is still a person loved by God. You can kill a person slowly by continually ridiculing him and making fun of him. Jesus is saying that one person has no right to insult another.

". . . And whoever says, 'You fool!' shall be liable to the hell of fire."

The Greek word which Jesus used for "You fool" is like our word "moron." It implies more than contempt. It means that you think another person is completely worthless, that you write him off as though he were dead. But no man is worthless in the eyes of God. Jesus proved that by his ministry. He touched the lives of many who were living in the gutters. His enemies sneered at his "eating with sinners," but this did not stop Jesus from seeking to help those who needed his forgiving love. The "hell of fire" that Jesus mentions is a phrase meant to indicate the worst of all judgment. It is a fair penalty, because when you consider a person worthless, you have killed him in your mind. And if you feel this way about him, you will not be reaching out to help him or to be nice to him as a follower of Christ should.

your own life is important

If we do not have the right to judge the lives of others, we likewise do not have the right to judge our own lives. We belong to God. We can't take the life that he gave us.

There are cases, of course, where a person in a fit of insanity might kill himself. God, in his infinite mercy and goodness, knows the condition of a man's mind, knows whether or not he is responsible for his actions. But the person who deliberately takes his own life, knowing full well what he is doing, is destroying his link with God.

One of the Bible's great tragedies is the story of Judas. Judas lived with Jesus for three years. He heard the same teachings that Peter did; he saw the same miracles of healing. What Judas did in betraying his Lord was really no worse a crime than Peter's denial or the other disciples scurrying to safety when Jesus was crucified. The tragedy was that Judas hanged himself in remorse. Peter and others were equally sorry, but they came back to Christ for forgiveness. Judas not only was judging himself, he was judging God. He was assuming that God would never help him again. But God always stands ready to help us, no matter how terrible our crimes.

Since our own lives are important, we have a responsibility to care for ourselves. Anything we do in excess, thereby injuring our bodies or minds, is wrong. Overeating can be harmful, as can overexercising or overworking. The use of alcohol or drugs in excess not only damages the self but, more significantly, can hurt others. Moreover, alcoholism and drug addiction, in affecting the mind as well as the body, prevent those who are addicted from being the responsible persons God intended them to be.

A Christian respects the life that God has put into his care. "Do you not know that your body is a temple of the Holy Spirit within you?" wrote Paul. "You are not your own; you were bought with a price. So glorify God in your body" (1 Corinthians 6:19-20).

keeping the fifth commandment

Obeying the Fifth Commandment is not as easy as it seems when you simply read the words, is it? The sacredness of human life,

which binds all men together as brothers under the fatherhood of God, shines through those four short words. It is because we love God that we love the people he has created.

This is where Luther begins in his interpretation of the commandment. Memorize his words: "We are to fear and love God so that we do not hurt our neighbor in any way, but help him in all his physical needs." To not hurt in any way is a big order. So is the command to help others in all their physical needs. Being a Christian is a full-time job.

You generally do not have to look very far to find someone who needs your help. Maybe you are the person who should be teaching younger children in your neighborhood good safety habits. Maybe you are able to do some simple repair work for older people near where you live to help them reduce accident hazards. Probably you have learned first aid techniques in scouting or in one of the youth clubs to which you belong. Being ready and able to help preserve life is the mark of a good citizen as well as the characteristic of a Christian.

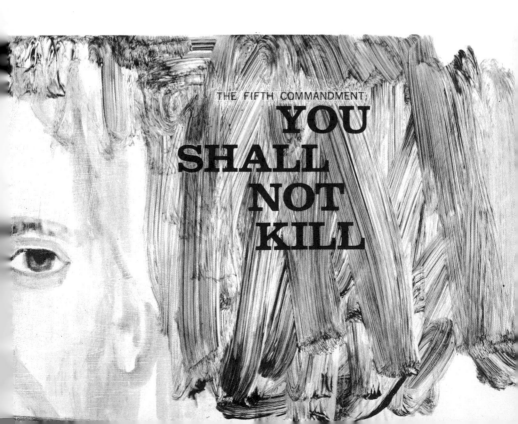

THE FIFTH COMMANDMENT

YOU SHALL NOT KILL

Let's look at some test cases of people caught in the web of their own selfishness or anger or greed. Do you think that any of them broke the Fifth Commandment? If so, how? What should they have done?

1. John Robinson owns a cheap apartment house that is nothing more than a slum. He refuses to repair sagging stairways and leaky pipes because he argues that he doesn't get enough money from rent to pay for the improvements.

2. Fred Jones is envious of Henry Moore's new racing bike. Before Henry came out of class one day, Fred cut partially through the brake line, hoping that Henry would have an accident.

3. Barbara Miller doesn't like Patty Adams because Patty is a very plain, awkward-looking girl. "My friends laugh at me if I'm friendly with Patty," says Barbara. "They say I must be hard up for company if I have to go around with that witch." Patty was deeply hurt when Barbara ignored her.

4. The boys know that Perry Benson has a weak heart. He was out of school for some time with rheumatic fever. Yet they taunt him and call him an old woman when he doesn't get into their rough games. Perry has been playing with them recently just to prove that he is as strong as they are.

5. "I hate you! I wish you were dead," Janey Thomas shouted at her brother when she was angry at him one day. She couldn't understand the terrible hurt look that came to his face.

6. An Oriental family moved into Bill Wilson's neighborhood. Bill said, "Well, they may live on our street, but we won't have anything to do with them. They're too different from us."

When we honor human life, we honor God himself, the creator of all life. But God doesn't expect us to sit back and admire the lives of others; he wants us to help the weak, to be a friend to the friendless, to do all we can to protect others. Harming another human being should be unthinkable for the Christian.

11

THE HOLINESS OF SEX

The theme of holiness runs all the way through the Ten Commandments. The word *holiness* means wholeness, purity, being worthy of the highest honor. God is holy and his gifts to us are, therefore, holy. For instance, all human life is the gift of God. Therefore, our task as God's sons is to help preserve and protect life.

TO READ AND THINK ABOUT
Genesis 2:20-25   God Creates the Family
John 2:1-11   Jesus Attends a Wedding
Matthew 19:3-6   Jesus' Teaching
Ephesians 5:22-33   Husband and Wife
Romans 12:1-2   Keep Yourself Holy
1 Corinthians 6:17-18   Shun Immorality
Philippians 4:8-9   Think About These Things

Sex, too, is God's creation. Man did not invent sex; it was God's idea. Therefore, we are to think of sex in terms of holiness. This includes accepting ourselves as sexual beings, male or female. It also means honoring the sex act between man and wife as part of God's plan for the creation of families. In God's eyes, sex is good, wholesome, beautiful, and right. He wants us to have this understanding of sex.

In simple terms, sex is the way God provides for: (*1*) *the most complete physical expression of love between a husband and wife in their marriage relationship*; and (*2*) *the creation of children born of that love.*

In order to keep people mindful of the proper place of sex in the human family, God gave a special law: You shall not commit adultery.

adultery

We usually use the term "adultery" to mean the sexual relations that a married man has with someone other than his wife, or a married woman has with someone other than her husband. This God does not want. From the very beginning of time, God planned to have one man and one woman form one family. No one has the right to break this oneness.

YOU SHALL NOT COMMIT ADULTERY

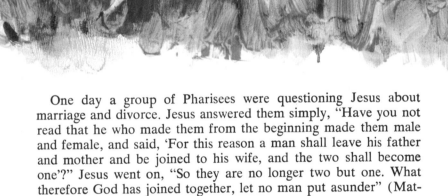

One day a group of Pharisees were questioning Jesus about marriage and divorce. Jesus answered them simply, "Have you not read that he who made them from the beginning made them male and female, and said, 'For this reason a man shall leave his father and mother and be joined to his wife, and the two shall become one'?" Jesus went on, "So they are no longer two but one. What therefore God has joined together, let no man put asunder" (Matthew 19:4-6).

The Sixth Commandment sounds as though it were intended only for married people. It doesn't have much to say to those who are not yet married. Or does it?

Adultery comes from the same root word that the verb "to adulterate" does. When you adulterate something, you corrupt it and make it impure.

A building contractor thought he would make a lot of money on a school contract. He used more sand in the mortar mix and less cement than the architect specified in order to make a few extra dollars. The building looked magnificent when it was completed, but the first violent windstorm in the fall sent it crumbling to the ground. Many children were injured. Because of the adulterated materials, the building was destroyed.

Your life is not unlike a building. Your thoughts and ideas, your habits and practices, help build your personality. You want to put only the best into the building of your life. You can adulterate the way you think about sex by the way you talk about it, for instance. If you make sex a "dirty" word, something that is unclean and disgusting, you will have a hard time building a Christian understanding of the beauty of marriage. Sometimes marriages fail simply because people have twisted and distorted their ideas of sex for so long that they don't know how to appreciate the sex relationship as God's gift.

luther's interpretation of the commandment

Luther thought that the idea of keeping sex holy in our thinking as well as in our practices was the real meaning of the Sixth Commandment. "We are to fear and love God so that in matters of sex our words and conduct are pure and honorable." Luther put these words first, and only then added, "And husband and wife love and respect each other." When you see how deep and broad the commandment actually is, you realize that it applies to all people. It doesn't matter whether they are young or old, married or unmarried. Everyone has the obligation to keep sex holy. Why? For the same reason that we should obey all the Commandments—because we love God. Sex is a gift of God and our love for God will not allow us to misuse his gifts.

keeping a clean mind

One of the hardest jobs a Christian faces is keeping his mind clean and pure. It is usually not much trouble for him to avoid doing the things that he knows are wrong; he wouldn't want to bring dishonor upon himself and his family. But in the secret places of his mind, he is often tempted to think about things that he knows are impure. But though we can hide our thoughts from our family and friends, we can't hide them from God. He knows what we are thinking. He also knows that we can break any commandment mentally, even though we give the impression to others that we are obedient.

Jesus made this point very clear in his Sermon on the Mount when he was discussing this commandment. "You have heard that it was said, 'You shall not commit adultery.' But I say to you that every one who looks at a woman lustfully has already committed adultery with her in his heart" (Matthew 5:27-28).

At one time, Jesus got very angry at some of the Pharisees who were going through the paces of being religious men but inwardly were full of ungodly passions. Jesus told them that they were like "whitewashed tombs, which outwardly appear beautiful, but within they are full of dead men's bones and all uncleanness" (Matthew 23:27). He was saying that a life could be like a handsome tomb in a cemetery, outwardly disguising its contents.

You can't prevent unclean thoughts from coming to your mind any more than you can avoid hearing unclean things and seeing unclean pictures. You live in a world that pays little attention to the Sixth Commandment. Wrong ideas of sex are all about you. Some magazines, books, records, and motion pictures deliberately describe and promote unchristian standards of sex. No, you can't prevent temptations from striking again and again. But you can do something about allowing those temptations to be turned into permanent possessions. You don't have to read, look at, or listen to things that you know are unholy.

Luther said, one time, "You can't prevent the birds from flying overhead, but you can prevent them from making nests in your hair."

honoring sex and christian marriage

It seems like a long time until you will be thinking of getting married and having a family of your own. Growing up is a slow process, for which you are probably thankful. You are not yet ready to think about spending the rest of your life with one person.

But you owe it to your God and to yourself to be the right kind of person now in preparation for that day. The greatest gift a person can give to another is himself. You want that self to be a worthy gift.

Sometimes you may have to face the jeers of your friends or the snide remarks of your enemies if you insist on living day by day as a son of God. Sometimes you may even have to stand alone for what you believe to be right. Sometimes you may have to struggle with impulses and urges that well up inside you. Being a disciple of Jesus Christ is never an easy matter. But in all these experiences, your trust in God will give you the strength to act properly.

Be forgiving of the weakness of others as you expect God to forgive you. We obey God's Commandments not so that we may be proud of our own accomplishments but to give honor to the God who loves us.

getting answers to your questions about sex

There are probably many questions about sex that you would like to have answered. Talk them over with your parents. They want to help you. They don't always know what questions are bothering you, so often they hesitate to give you information. There is no shame connected with talking about sex. We want to understand the nature of God's wonderful gift to us.

Your pastor is also ready to help you. He can guide you in developing your Christian attitude toward sex, love, and marriage. It's easy to get confused about the real place of sex in life when you depend on the half-truths and distorted ideas of sex that you hear from time to time from unreliable sources. Go to those mature people whom you trust for straight answers.

12

CARING FOR POSSESSIONS

We give thee but thine own,
Whate'er the gift may be;
All that we have is thine alone,
A trust, O Lord, from thee. (*SBH* 544)

Do you know this familiar hymn? The words have a lot to say about our possessions. The verse embodies these two important ideas:

1. Everything we have belongs to God.

God's great generosity is unbelievable. Although everything in the world belongs to him, he gives us all that we have—not because of any merit or worthiness on our part, but because he loves us.

He gives us life and the world in which to live. Although it is we who carve toy sailboats from the wood of a tree or build rocket ships from the metals mined from the ground, we can only do so because God has given us the raw materials. He trusts us to use his gifts well.

TO READ AND THINK ABOUT

Psalm 24   The Earth Is the Lord's
Deuteronomy 22:1-3   Returning Lost Things
Leviticus 25:35-36   Caring for the Needy
2 Thessalonians 3:10-12   Work
Luke 16:1-13   The Unjust Steward
Matthew 25:14-30   Possessions in Trust
1 Peter 4:7-11   Advice for Stewards

---

2. Every gift we give to God is returning something that already belongs to him.

As Christians, we cannot help but live with a keen consciousness of God's gifts. We honor our parents because God gave them to us. We respect human life because it is God-given. We keep our understanding of sex holy because it is God's gift to the family. But don't misunderstand the words of the hymn. We can't give God's gifts back to him literally. He has no human needs. Giving to God means using all that we have for the fulfillment of his will. And the greatest gift we can give to God is ourselves. When we become disciples of Christ we do just that—give ourselves back to God.

In some congregations, this hymn is sung during The Service

following the offering. Many people, therefore, get the idea that the words refer only to our gifts of money to God. Actually, these mean little unless we also dedicate our lives to God's service. This means holding all God's gifts with honor, using them for his glory and for the benefit of others. There is no room for selfishness here.

stealing

Stealing is a civil crime everywhere you go in the world. All governments have laws to protect their people from thieves. Most countries agree, however, that the punishment for stealing depends upon the value of what has been stolen. A man who robs a bank receives a stiffer prison sentence than the man who takes a loaf of bread from the corner grocery. This leads many people to think that stealing on a large scale is wrong but that petty pilfering is all right if you can get away with it. We may even cheer the exploits of a Robin Hood, arguing that because he stole from the rich and gave to the poor, he was a hero.

As far as God is concerned, all stealing is wrong. No one has the right to take anything that belongs to someone else.

something for nothing

One reason people steal is because they want something for nothing. It would be wonderful if you could get all the things you wanted without having to work and save for them. But it seldom happens. The story of Aladdin and his magic lamp belongs in the *Arabian Nights*.

You have read about swindlers who trick people into buying shares in oil wells that don't exist. It's an old racket. It seems that many people are willing to take a chance on anything that promises them quick, easy money. So many rackets exist today that most city police departments have racket squads to deal with swindlers. But swindlers must have victims if they are to stay in business.

Anybody is an easy victim if he is eager to get something for nothing. That's why gambling has become big business. Some states make it legal for people to risk their money on a turn of the wheel or on the speed of a horse. Slot machines and turkey raffles, card games of chance and bingo—they are really all the same thing. Gambling flourishes when people forget that their money and all their possessions are held in trust for God. You may think that taking a chance for a quarter on a car auctioned off by a local service club isn't a bad thing. After all, the service club is using the money it makes for the benefit of some worthy cause like providing musical instruments for an orphanage. But couldn't they have made more money for the orphanage by interesting people in helping? The worst thing about this form of gambling, innocent as it seems, is that it still promotes the "something-for-nothing" idea.

the christian attitude toward property

Don't think that God was opposed to the idea of our having things to call our own. Jesus never said that possessions are wrong. He did point out, however, that possessions and the desire for possessions can get in the way of our giving ourselves completely to God. This was the tragedy of the rich young ruler who had many possessions that he could not give up. The ruler wanted to become a disciple of Jesus, but his possessions got in his way.

God gave us a world of things in which to live. He wants us to use them well for our own benefit and for the benefit of others. He also expects us to respect the property rights of other people. All this we do because, as the psalmist wrote, 'The earth is the LORD's and the fulness thereof" (Psalm 24:1a).

Luther summed up these ideas when he wrote his interpretation of the Seventh Commandment, "We are to fear and love God so that we do not take our neighbor's money or property, or get them in any dishonest way, but help him to improve and protect his property and means of making a living."

Luther felt that God trusts all of us, as his sons, to take good care of the things we and others possess.

christian stewardship

In our church we use the term "stewardship" to explain the trust God places in us to care for his world. In biblical times, a steward was a man employed on a large estate to handle the affairs of the owner. The steward would manage the affairs, supervise the servants, and keep the accounts. The steward was always responsible to the owner for what he did.

Jesus told many parables about stewards, using them as an example of the way we should treat both God and our fellowmen. Read his story of the unjust steward (Luke 16:1-13).

A good steward is one who not only takes care of his own responsibilities but respects the rights of others. Suppose you saw your friend's bike standing out in the rain. Would you steal it? Certainly not. You would help him get the bike undercover and wipe it off so that it wouldn't rust. That is Christian stewardship, too.

If we are wise stewards of our possessions, we always have more than we need of the good things of life. Therefore, we give to the work of the church; we share with those less fortunate than we are. In this way we show our thankfulness to God for his many gifts.

Keeping the Seventh Commandment is nothing more than being aware that we are stewards of God in all that we have. If we keep that idea always in mind, we will take good care of our possessions and help our neighbors protect and care for their belongings as well.

THE SEVENTH COMMANDMENT:
YOU
SHALL NOT STEAL

13

SPEAKING THE TRUTH IN LOVE

A man is on trial for murder. The courtroom is packed. An eye-witness to the crime is taking the witness stand. The bailiff of the court asks the witness to swear that he will tell "the truth, the whole truth, and nothing but the truth." He agrees. Tension fills the air as everyone waits for the testimony. A man's reputation, perhaps even his life, hangs in the balance.

TO READ AND THINK ABOUT

James 3:2-12   Taming Your Tongue
Proverbs 15:1-7   Wise Speaking
Psalm 139:1-6   God Knows What We Say
Ephesians 4:15-16, 25   Speaking the Truth in Love
Ephesians 4:29-32   Don't Lie or Slander
John 14:5-7   Jesus Is the Truth
1 Corinthians 5:6-8   Sincerity and Truth

Suppose the witness lies. Or suppose he only tells part of the truth. He could cause the defendant to receive an unjust verdict from the court. Lying under oath is a crime; it is called perjury. A person who perjures himself in court is liable to get punished severely, and he deserves to be. Truth is an essential part of our judiciary system. Without truth, there can be no justice.

Unless men are able to respect and trust each other, unless they are able to depend on each other's truthfulness, no society can last. The same kind of honor and respect is necessary to hold families together; to make friendships last; and to enable people of different nationalities, races, and religions to work together in peace.

The necessity of speaking the truth and living by the truth is as important in our highly technical civilization as it was among primitive people a long time ago. God knew that men must have a respect for the reputation of one another. Therefore, he built truth into the Ten Commandments.

At first reading, the Eighth Commandment seems to apply only to a courtroom situation, but this is a narrow interpretation. The ancient Jews also interpreted the commandment narrowly. They understood these words to apply to the way they treated each other, but not necessarily to the way they were to treat those who were not Jewish. They felt that the commandment covered such things as "framing" a neighbor for a crime he didn't commit and bribing others to tell lies, as well as lying themselves. They felt that Jews should be able to trust one another because they belonged to God's chosen people. The wise author of Proverbs wrote, "He who speaks the truth gives honest evidence, but a false witness utters deceit" (Proverbs 12:17).

Jesus taught that the Commandments applied to our dealings with all men. He wanted the Jews to realize that they were not the only people of God. God created all men. One of the tragedies of Jesus' trial is that hatred against him rose to such a fever pitch that false witnesses were employed to condemn him. Some of the Jews broke a cherished commandment in their vain attempt to still the voice of Jesus.

loving your neighbor

The only possible way of keeping the Eighth Commandment is by loving people, by caring what happens to them, by doing what you can to help them. You may not always like what people do, but you are under the orders of God to love and respect them. John put the whole matter before us in words that cannot be misunderstood: "If any one says, 'I love God,' and hates his brother, he is a liar; for he who does not love his brother whom he has seen, cannot love God whom he has not seen. And this commandment we have from him, that he who loves God should love his brother also" (1 John 4:20-21).

This Christian idea of loving all men is behind Luther's explanation of the Eighth Commandment. Luther wrote, "We are to fear and love God so that we do not betray, slander, or lie about our neighbor, but defend him, speak well of him, and explain his actions in the kindest way." That's a big order! Let's look at Luther's interpretation more closely, beginning with the negative side.

ways of lying

In one of his books, Mark Twain said that there are 869 ways to tell a lie. There may indeed be that many; there may be more. People invent new ways to twist and distort the truth every day. A newspaper may print only half the facts of a news event, giving you a wrong impression of what really happened. A politician, in his campaign speech, may deliberately misinterpret his opponent's actions in order to get more votes for himself. Advertisements tell you that you will have all kinds of friends and admirers if you use a certain hair lotion. It's hard to know what to believe at times.

The problem of lying is even more complicated because people

try to distinguish between "the big lie" and "the little white lie," between nasty rumors and idle gossip. Yet, every time you twist the truth, someone or something can be damaged. The commandment isn't as concerned with the damage you do to yourself when you lie as it is with the damage you can do to the reputation of someone else. Luther says we should not "betray, slander, or lie" about our neighbor. Let's look closely at these three words:

To Lie: This means to spread false stories about someone, to cast doubts about his character, to accuse him of doing or saying things he didn't do or say.

To Slander: This means to add deliberate evil intent to your lying. When you slander someone, you are trying to hurt his reputation. You want him to suffer. We usually use the word *slander* to refer to spoken lies against someone, and the word *libel* if these untruths are printed.

To Betray: This means to be a false friend. You betray a person if you take a personal, private confidence a friend has told you and make it public. You may expose him to ridicule and scorn by repeating things you know simply because you were a close friend. The betrayer is a "false witness" because he has broken his responsibility to be trustworthy.

YOU SHALL NOT BEAR FALSE WITNESS AGAINST YOUR NEIGHBOR

Actually, any time we hurt someone by untruth through what we say or write, or even through our actions—every time we are untrustworthy—we break the bond of the Eighth Commandment.

gossip

One word that Luther didn't mention specifically was gossip. Yet gossip can be one of the most devilish ways of lying. Even pronouncing the word *gossip* requires us to utter the "hissing" sound of a snake. People who have the habit of gossiping probably seldom think of themselves as liars. But they often are. What else can you call someone who deliberately passes on false information or half-truths? The gossiper seldom checks the facts; he often adds some touches of his own to the reports he hears.

The worst thing about gossip is that it usually concentrates on a person's failures and faults. Gossip delights in tearing people down and discrediting their good points. Notice how the gossiper often begins: "You know that Jack is a good student, but did you know that he . . ." "Now, don't get me wrong, I like Sally, but . . ." "Jim thinks he's hot stuff, but let me tell you . . ." "Jeanie asked me not to tell, but I know you'll keep a secret, so . . ." Gossip, you see, can include all the verbs Luther used—lie, slander, betray.

acting a lie

Don't think that bearing false witness is limited to speaking lies or betraying a trust. The way you speak the truth, the inflection in your voice, may create the effect of a lie. Suppose you said, "Tom never cheats (pause) in history class." You could give others the impression that Tom does cheat in his other classes. Actually, you are using the dramatic quality of your voice to act a lie.

Another way you can act a lie is to make yourself seem to be something that you are not. You may pretend to be friendly in order to get someone to do you a favor. Then, when the favor is done, you drop his friendship. Think of the many times you try to fool your parents, your teachers, your pastor, even your closest friends into thinking that you are different from what you really are. If you do very much of this, it will be hard for anyone to get to know the real you. Be honest with yourself. Then you will be more likely to be honest with others in all your dealings with them.

judge not

Why do people lie? They do it for a lot of reasons, some of which are too complicated to understand. A few common reasons are: because they are selfish and want to make themselves appear important in the eyes of others; because they are insecure and afraid their real selves aren't good enough; because they want to hurt someone they don't like; because they want to "get back at" people they feel deserve punishment.

Whatever the reasons, whether lying is done to build yourself up or to tear someone else down, every lie is the result of a faulty decision, a decision that does not reflect the love of God. If we love God, then we are bound to love our fellowmen, no matter what their faults. We do not have the right to judge them, to decide that they are unworthy of our love. Likewise, we have no right to judge ourselves. If we love God, then we know that he loves us and accepts us. Who are we, then, to decide that we aren't good enough?

It is important to remember that it is not enough simply not to betray, lie about, or slander our fellowmen. We must act positively in the other direction; we must love them. That is why Luther adds the second part to his explanation of the Eighth Commandment, saying that we should "defend him (our neighbor), speak well of him, and explain his actions in the kindest way."

love in action

God puts you on the side of your neighbor, instead of against him. God puts you in the position, as his son, of defending and encouraging your neighbor. He wants you to see the best in your fellowmen, to be kind and thoughtful in interpreting their actions. This is the only way that love can act.

When Jesus looked into the hearts of people, he saw them for what they could be. He saw the possibilities of greatness in Peter. Even when Peter failed him over and over again, even when Peter lied during Jesus' trial and said he never knew this carpenter from Galilee, Jesus was still willing to forgive him. Jesus' friendship and firm trust spurred Peter into becoming a great leader of the early Christian church.

In seeing the best in people and helping them keep good reputations, you are acting toward them as Christ would. You are putting aside your selfishness, your personal likes and dislikes, and beginning to think in terms of helping others.

speaking the truth in love

One way of helping others is always to speak the truth with kindness and love. Hank may be far from good-looking. Still you wouldn't say to him, "You are really ugly." This may be the truth, but why hurt Hank's feelings? He doesn't need to be told it; it won't help him if you do. Sometimes consideration for the welfare of others makes you keep silent. If you tell Karen that she is a lousy tennis player, she may be so crushed that she will give up the game altogether. What have you accomplished? On the other hand, offering Karen the help she needs to improve her game by speaking the truth tactfully, with love, is another matter.

Here are four questions to ask yourself whenever you have doubts about what to say either to others or about others:

1. Is it true?
2. Is it kind?
3. Is it necessary?
4. Is it helpful to them?

Part Four

God Expects Obedience

14

CONTROLLING DESIRES

Most people want some sense of limit to their lives. They want to know how far they can go in their freedom as individuals and where they begin trespassing on the rights of others. The Ten Commandments help us see where the limits in our lives are.

TO READ AND THINK ABOUT

Luke 11:37 41   What Is Within Counts
Jeremiah 17:9-11   The Heart Is Deceitful
Micah 2:1-5   What Happens to Covetous People
Luke 12:15-21   Beware of Covetousness
Colossians 3:5, 10   Covetousness Is Idolatry
Romans 7:7-12   The Law Is Holy
1 Timothy 6:6-10   Contentment

The first three commandments talk about God in your life. They also describe the limits in your relationship with God. You are not to make your own gods, or crowd him out, or play God yourself. Instead, you are to put God first in all things and worship him as your heavenly Father. Each of these three commandments suggests a line that you dare not cross without damaging the fellowship you have with God.

Commandments Four through Eight explain the bonds that unite you with others. Here is God's Law telling you what he expects of you as his child. In these five commandments, God has shown us the limits to our relationships with other people as they apply to the family and sex and property, indeed, even around every man's life and reputation. He says to you, "You must respect, honor, and protect what I have given."

The Ninth and Tenth Commandments make certain other limitations in our lives stand out clearly. These commandments ask us to preserve and protect that which belongs to our neighbors. They do so by asking us to limit ourselves. We are directed to look searchingly and honestly at our inner drives—the desires and wants and ambitions that are so much a part of our personalities. As Christians, we have no right to desire anything that we should not have or that rightfully belongs to another. We have to learn to control our desires.

According to the dictionary, *coveting* means seeking for, or longing for, something that belongs to another person. Some churches make these last two commandments one, saying that it doesn't matter what you covet, coveting is wrong. Luther, and others, felt that there were two distinct commandments: one in terms of property and possessions (the Ninth); and the other in terms of living things like family, servants, and animals (the Tenth).

the ninth commandment

These commandments do not necessarily refer to breaking the laws of community or country. They speak to the way some people may bend and twist the laws in order to gain someone else's possessions. A businessman wants a certain farm because he happens to know that there are rich mineral deposits in the land. He buys the land for a fair price from the farmer, but doesn't tell him about the real value of his property. As a result, the businessman

makes a large profit and the farmer loses what should have been rightfully his. Everything was perfectly legal—but hardly Christian!

The Ninth Commandment, says Luther, means that "we are to fear and love God so that we do not desire to get our neighbor's possessions by scheming, or by pretending to have a right to them, but always help him keep what is his." Luther was quite aware of what coveting could lead to, and he makes it clear that merely having the law on our side does not make such actions right in the sight of God.

the tenth commandment

The Tenth Commandment is like the Ninth, in that it is possible to stay within the law and still manage to break the commandment. If we try to win the affections and loyalty of those closely connected with our neighbor, so that they willingly break their ties with him, we are crossing the limits God has put around the neighbors' rights, as well as the limits he has set on our own actions.

Luther said, "We are to fear and love God so that we do not

THE NINTH COMMANDMENT:

YOU SHALL NOT COVET YOUR NEIGHBORS HOUSE

THE TENTH COMMANDMENT:

YOU SHALL NOT COVET YOUR NEIGHBOR'S WIFE OR HIS MANSERVANT, OR HIS MAIDSERVANT, OR HIS CATTLE OR ANYTHING THAT IS YOUR NEIGHBOR'S

tempt or coax away from our neighbor his wife or his workers, but encourage them to remain loyal." Notice how Luther always emphasizes helping instead of hurting, working for our neighbor instead of against him.

At this point, you are probably thinking that the problem of wife- or husband-stealing belongs to grown-ups, and you are right. So does the matter, usually, of inviting another person's servants to work for you. You probably don't have a large enough allowance to afford even one servant. But the commandment still speaks to you.

Suppose you covet the closeness and trust two brothers, Jack and Jerry, have in each other. They always seem to have fun together; they like being with each other. You would like to be friends with Jerry, but you don't like Jack knowing everything you say or do. You would even like to take Jack's place in Jerry's life. So you try very hard to turn Jerry against his brother. Would God approve of your actions?

Or consider the matter of animals—the Tenth Commandment mentions them specifically. You can steal the affection an animal has for his owner. Take the case of Jill, who coveted the new puppy of her neighbor, Mrs. Morton.

Jill went over to the Morton yard almost every day to play with the pup. Mrs. Morton welcomed her and permitted her to come as often as she liked. Jill took advantage of her freedom. She taught the pup to follow her and rewarded him with a piece of candy or a dog biscuit when he did. She petted him so often that he came to accept her as someone close to him. When the pup followed her home one day, she rewarded him with a plate of food; she kept him for several hours before she returned him. You know what happened. When the dog grew older, he wouldn't stay at the Morton's; he went over to Jill's house every chance he got. Eventually, Mrs. Morton gave Jill the dog; she didn't know what else to do. The woman never knew the trick that had been played on her.

desires, right and wrong

Don't get the idea that it is wrong to have desires. Wanting to have things, wanting to do things, wanting to be a better person— these are normal human urges. God asks only that we control our desires. He wants us to live happily and contentedly within the boundaries he has set.

To want a transistor radio is one thing; to want the particular portable radio that Henry has, is something else. In the first case, you may save up your money until you can buy the model you want. In the second, you may try all sorts of schemes to get Henry's radio away from him.

Take another example. Margie is a good piano player. The

86

gang likes to gather around the piano and sing when she plays. You would also like to play the piano well and provide music for group singing. That's fine. But suppose the real reason you practice hard and long is not just so that you can play well, but so that you can take Margie's place in the affections of the crowd. You are jealous of her popularity; you would like to shove her to the sidelines so you could move into the limelight. That's a different story, isn't it? You see, our motives tell us whether our desires are right or wrong.

housecleaning

The last two commandments want us to examine ourselves, to see our unholy desires for what they are. Every springtime, and possibly also in the fall, your mother gives the house a thorough cleaning. The junk, the things she no longer wants or can use, is usually thrown out on the trash pile. Good riddance! Self-examination is like going through a spiritual housecleaning, ridding ourselves of the desires that should be discarded.

Here are some of the names for the rubbish we collect, the unholy desires that torment us:

Envy: Envy is what you feel when you cannot bear to see someone have something you do not have, when you are miserable because of another person's success or talents or possessions. It is a short step from envy to covetousness—wanting to get for yourself what someone else has.

Greed: Greed is unreasonable desire for material things. You can be greedy in terms of food or clothing as well as in terms of money and possessions. Greed can easily become covetousness when you value what you want more than you value the rights of others.

Resentment: Resentment is a feeling of anger at what you think are hurts or wrongs. Resentment can lead to covetousness if you think that someone has gotten a "better deal" than you have—if you think they have gotten something you deserved—and you feel you should have it.

There is only one thing to do with your evil desires. Pull them out into the daylight so you can see them for what they are. Then ask God to help you sweep them out of your life.

Coveting, in all its many forms, is not only damaging to your relationships with other people, it spoils your relationship with God. Coveting can take over your life and make you forget about God. We should always be on guard against it: for the Christian, every day should be housecleaning day.

coveting leads to other evils

So far we have discussed the commandments about coveting without specifically mentioning their relation to other commandments. One of the worst things about coveting is that it can lead us to break any or all of the other commandments. Jesus told us that evil comes from the heart. What we think and feel often determine what we do.

Let's look at three famous examples from the Old Testament to see how coveting can lead to other evils:

1. Cain and Abel (Read Genesis 4:1-16.)

From the very dawn of history comes this story of Cain, the farmer, who was envious of the blessings his brother Abel, a shepherd, received from God and resentful because he had not received them. In insane hatred, Cain killed his brother.

2. David and Bathsheba (Read 2 Samuel 11.)

David wanted the wife of Uriah, one of his soldiers. Not only did David commit adultery with Bathsheba, but because he coveted her, he made plans for Uriah to be placed at the front of the battlelines so that he would be killed.

3. Ahab and Naboth (Read 1 Kings 21.)

Naboth had a vineyard beside the royal palace of King Ahab. Ahab wanted the vineyard to make a vegetable garden, but Naboth refused to sell. In order to get possession of the vineyard, Ahab's wife, Jezebel, suggested that they employ false witnesses to accuse Naboth of cursing both God and the king. As a result, Naboth was put to death for his "crimes," and Ahab got the vineyard.

These are terrible stories. They describe the very worst in human behavior. The Bible makes no attempt to "whitewash" anyone, farmer or king. This honesty is immensely valuable, because unless people see how horrible sin and its effects can be, they may not be concerned about their own sinfulness. At the same time that it tells about sins of people, the Bible shows how these same people can be changed. God's love and forgiveness are always ready to help those who are truly sorry for what they have done. Think of how much heartache and guilt Cain and David, Ahab and Jezebel could have avoided if they had gotten rid of their unholy desires before they acted on them.

the parable of the haunted house

Jesus once told a parable about a haunted house. This house is not an old gray mansion with flapping shutters and leaky roof where spooks and hobgoblins are thought to come out at night. The haunted house of Jesus' tale is a human mind.

The parable is about a man with an "unclean spirit." (The people of Jesus' day used the term "unclean spirit" to refer to any evil which seemed to possess a person.) Somehow the man gets rid of this evil spirit. The spirit then wanders around looking for rest, said Jesus. But it finds no place to settle down; so it goes back to the man and finds that the man's mind is all cleaned up, swept clean, put in order. There is nothing in this clean emptiness! Seeing this, the spirit rushes out and gets seven other spirits more evil than himself. They all enter that man's mind and live there. "And the last state of that man becomes worse than the first," concluded Jesus. (Read Matthew 12:43-45.)

Do you get Jesus' point? It is not enough simply to houseclean our minds of sinful desires, we have to put something good in their place. Luther understood this truth clearly. That's why he said that the last two commandments mean that we should help our neighbor "keep what is his."

Instead of envy, we should put in our hearts a desire to rejoice at a neighbor's good fortune. To share his happiness in a new possession or a new honor is to forbid envy to raise its head. Instead of greed, we need to cultivate a feeling of thankfulness for what we have. This brings contentment, and contentment is a priceless blessing. What all this really means is that evil desires need to be replaced with the greatest power for good in the world—the love of God. For if we love God, we will love our fellowmen for his sake. And if we love our fellowmen, we will be truly free of coveting.

15

"THE CORD THAT TIES THE WREATH TOGETHER"

When you compare the text of the Ten Commandments in Exodus 20 with the way Martin Luther arranged the Commandments in the *Small Catechism*, you will notice something odd. Luther took some of the verses related to the First Commandment (verses 5 and 6) and placed them after all the Commandments, as an answer to the question "What does God say of all these commandments?" Do you agree that these verses seem to fit there?

He says: "I, the LORD your God, am a jealous God, visiting the iniquity of the fathers upon the children to the third and fourth generation of those who hate me, but showing steadfast love to thousands of those who love me and keep my commandments."

TO READ AND THINK ABOUT

Deuteronomy 6:4-9   *Never Forget the Commandments*
Leviticus 26:14-45   *Punishment of Disobedience*
Ezekiel 18:19-32   *God Is Just*
Romans 6:12-23   *Yield Yourself to God*
1 Timothy 4:7-10   *Train Yourself in Godliness*
Ephesians 5:1-10   *Be Imitators of God*
1 John 3:19-24   *Keeping God's Commandments*

These words mean, says Luther, that "God warns that he will punish all who break these commandments. Therefore we are to fear his wrath and not disobey him. But he promises grace and every blessing to all who keep these commandments. Therefore we are to love and trust him, and gladly do what he commands."

Just as the opening statement of the Ten Commandments, "I am the LORD your God," introduces all the Commandments, so verses 5 and 6 tie all the Commandments together. No commandment is more important than another; they are all linked together.

the cord

On one occasion Luther commented that these verses we have just examined are like "the cord that ties the wreath together." If you think of a holly wreath at Christmastime, you will see what

Luther means. To make a holly wreath, you need to take the individual leaves and tie them together in a circle with wire or cord. When you have put a red satin ribbon on the wreath and hung the wreath on your front door, you no longer think of it as a collection of little pieces. It is one object.

So God's statement about punishment and reward takes the Commandments, each concerned with a particular relationship with God or other people, and binds them into a whole. Every limit God has set on your life is important. It is not a matter of obeying only those commandments that appeal to us, and ignoring the others. If we let God come into our lives, if we accept Jesus Christ as our Lord, then we accept all of God's will for us cheerfully. We know that he wills only good for us; that his Law is designed to help us find all that is good and lasting in life.

the jealous God

When God says, "I, the LORD your God, am a jealous God," he tells you something very important about himself. God uses the word "jealous" because he will not put up with rivals; he wants no other gods in your life. You belong to him. He will do everything he can to remind you of that fact.

Most people think jealousy is a bad mental attitude to have. A jealous person is usually worried about competition. You can be jealous of another person's good looks or his athletic skill or his high marks in class. This kind of jealousy means that you want what he has; when you feel this way, jealousy becomes an unreasonable form of envy. But this is only one meaning of jealousy. It can also mean thinking so highly of something that you want to protect it. People of a free nation *should* be jealous of their freedoms and try to preserve them for everyone who lives there. You *should* be jealous of your family name, so that you do nothing to bring dishonor upon it. In this sense, God is jealous about the people whom he loves—and he loves every person who has ever lived. God wants them for his own; he wants them to live so close to him that they can talk to him personally as "Our Father who art in heaven."

Don't ever get a picture of God as some kindly old gentleman, living far-off in a kingdom of silver clouds, who clucks his tongue when you do wrong and then winks at your sins. God is kind, and he is deeply hurt when you wrong him or your fellowmen. But he doesn't sit back with folded hands letting you go your own way. He enters right into the stream of life to fight for you. He sends his Son Jesus Christ to be your personal Lord. He tells you of his love for you over and over again. God is jealous of your relationship with him; he will do everything to help you accept him as your God—

except force you to do it. He only wants your love and devotion when you give it freely.

God is always just in all his dealings with men. He allows you to make up your own mind about him. He tells you that you have freedom to say either, "Yes, I want you for my God," or "No, I don't." But he wants you also to be sure that you understand the consequences of your choice. Therefore, he gives you both a warning and a promise.

the warning

The warning is expressed in the words "visiting the iniquity of the fathers upon the children to the third and fourth generation of those who hate me." These are difficult words to understand.

Iniquity originally meant not being fair or just. It is a synonym for sin, evil, injustice, the wrongs men do. A lie is an iniquity as much as a murder. Concentrating on unclean thoughts offends God as much as your attempts to take things that do not belong to you. Whenever you put God in second place in your life or force him out of your life altogether, you are guilty of iniquity.

God, who is holy, will not allow unholiness to go unpunished. Luther says, "God warns that he will punish all who break these commandments. Therefore, we are to fear his wrath and not disobey him."

God "visits the iniquity" of men upon them. This is one way of saying that God allows men to punish themselves. When you stop and think about it, God doesn't need to punish us; we do a very good job of punishing ourselves. When you do something that you know is wrong, you feel guilty. Whatever joy you expected from your misdeed is gone; the heavy weight of guilt will not allow you to be content. You have no true inner peace until you know that you have been forgiven.

God is thoughtful and fair with us. He gives us fair warning about our response to his will. When we break his Commandments, we have to face him for judgment. There is no hiding place where we can escape him. We can't even hide in the privacy of our own hearts; he knows when we break his Commandments mentally.

Think of the three Old Testament examples of covetousness that we talked about in the last chapter. We didn't talk about the end of the stories: Each of these men who had committed a crime against God and against his fellowmen had to face God's judgment.

1. Cain: God himself confronted Cain and asked him where his brother was. Thinking that he could lie to God, Cain answered, "I do not know; am I my brother's keeper?" But God, knowing the truth, told Cain that he had forfeited his chance for a happy, contented life, and that he would be punished by having the thing he loved best, farming, become a heavy burden. (Read Genesis 4:9-13.)

2. *David:* Because he was king of Israel, David thought he could do anything he wanted—even something as wrong as having Uriah killed in battle, so that he could marry Uriah's wife, Bathsheba. God sent the prophet Nathan to accuse David and bring him to his senses. Unlike Cain, who was unrepentant, David realized what he had done and was truly sorry. For this reason, his punishment was not as severe as Cain's but, even so, he still had to take the consequences. (Read 2 Samuel 12:1-15 to see the ingenuity Nathan used in making David realize his sin.)

3. *Ahab:* Ahab got Naboth's vineyard, but he was unable to enjoy it, because God sent the prophet Elijah to him to remind him of his crimes and to describe the terrible punishment that awaited him. He did repent his deed, and God therefore made his punishment less harsh. But, like David, he still did not escape punishment. (Read 1 Kings 21:17-24.)

"to the third and fourth generation"

It sounds cruel for God to say that he will visit "the iniquity of the fathers upon the children to the third and fourth generation of those who hate me." This looks as if God will punish not only the fathers, but even innocent children for the wrongs of their fathers. It is certainly true that a man's children and even his grandchildren may suffer for his sins. But this is because he brought the punishment upon himself and his family; it is a consequence of his actions, not of God's.

Suppose there was a settler in the early days of the Old West who built a home out of the wilderness. In order to do so, he forced Indians to leave the area, fencing off their hunting lands to graze his cattle and driving them from their tenting ground by a cool stream. Suppose this same man trained his children and his grandchildren to hate Indians, to say "The only good Indian is a dead Indian." Years later, when a small town had grown in the place of that first house and many people had moved to the new territory, the Indians went on the warpath. They attacked the town, burning the buildings, killing all the men, taking the women and children captive. Look how many people suffered because one man was thoughtless, selfish, and unkind.

The sins of that pioneer father were passed on from generation to generation like a deadly disease. His prejudice against the Indians had to be taught carefully to his children; they were not born with hatred of another man because his skin was a different color or because, living in a buffalo-hide tent, he smelled unpleasant to them.

But even if a child had refused to believe that all Indians were bad, it would not have prevented his being killed in the massacre. He was the victim of someone else's iniquity.

Seldom does a wrong affect only the wrongdoer. Suppose a parent breaks the speed laws and shows contempt for traffic lights when he drives. Even though he may not realize it, he is training his children to be poor drivers; he is not teaching them proper respect for the law. But don't think that this applies only to parents. You can set a bad example for a friend, or for a younger brother or sister. They may have to share in the punishment that only you really deserve.

"those who hate me"

"Those who hate me" is the key phrase in understanding what God means in the passage we are studying. You cannot have two gods in your life at the same time. Whenever you forget that God is your God and that you owe him love and trust and obedience, you are on dangerous ground. It is just one more step to turning against God and saying that he has no business trying to run your life. What else is this but hatred for God? Forgetting God, turning against God, hating God—all bring darkness into life.

Jesus described himself as the "light" for those living in darkness. He said, "I am the light of the world; he who follows me will not walk in darkness, but will have the light of life" (John 8:12). John commented earlier in his Gospel, "For everyone who does evil hates the light, and does not come to the light, lest his deeds should be exposed" (John 3:20).

Have you ever, when you were out walking in the woods, picked up a rotting log and seen all the insects and other creatures that went scurrying off in all directions? They were accustomed to living in darkness and couldn't stand the sudden light. This is the way people are who have gone against God, said Jesus. They can't stand the light of truth; they have to run away. People who live in the darkness, who insist on their own selfish ways, find themselves hating God and Jesus and all that reminds them of holiness. They don't want to know how wrong they are. But God wants them to know they are wrong and to know that punishment will come when they break the Commandments. He tells them so when he warns of punishment for "those who hate me."

the promise

God's words of warning are like one side of a coin. On the other side is God's promise that he will show "steadfast love to thousands of those who love me and keep my commandments." Both the warning and the promise are part of God's love. He protects what is right and good and decent.

94

The phrase "steadfast love" stands for mercy, for forgiveness, for dependability. When you say something is steadfast, you mean that it holds fast and firm. Steadfast love is firm, steady, unchanging. God's love is constant. You can depend on that. In fact, you can't stop God from loving you; you can only block the effectiveness of that love in your life. The writer of Hebrews says of Jesus Christ that he is, "the same yesterday and today and for ever" (Hebrews 13:8). He could also have said the same thing about God. God never changes.

One of the fine word-pictures that Jesus drew of God was the image of the father in the Parable of the Prodigal Son. No matter how far away from home the son went, no matter how many were his sins, the father never stopped loving him. When the boy finally came to his senses, was sorry for what he had done, and returned home, his father rushed out of the house to meet him, threw his arms about him, and welcomed him home (Luke 15:11-24). God is like that father, Jesus was saying, always ready to welcome his erring son home.

The New Testament frequently uses the word "grace" to mean all that we have said about "steadfast love." That's why Luther says that God "promises grace and every blessing to all who keep these commandments."

It is impossible to describe the greatness of God's grace or to count up all his blessings. God gives us so much. One of the wonderful truths about God is that he keeps on giving us all that he has as long as we live. And even the end of our lives does not end the gifts. He has promised eternal life to all who love him.

the obligation of obedience

Luther asks us to "gladly do what he (God) commands" because we "love and trust him." This is the secret of real obedience, accepting God's will because we want to, not because we have to.

It is a strange truth about human nature that, generally, whenever we know that we must do something, we rebel. We don't like to carry out orders. This is true at home, in the classroom, everywhere. Sometimes people break the law deliberately because they don't want someone to tell them to "Keep Off the Grass" or "Keep Quiet —Hospital Zone."

When you love someone, however, the whole picture changes. Then you want to do gladly what this person asks of you. You love him so much that you would do anything for him. Luther reminds you that, when you remember how much you love God, you want to keep his Commandments as part of his will for your life.

A Portfolio of Pictures of Christ

Rembrandt **HEAD OF CHRIST**

In the minds of many, Rembrandt van Rijn (1606-1669), a Dutch Protestant, is one of the world's greatest religious artists. In his portraits Rembrandt exhibits a masterly skill in painting outward physical details; he also captures the inner spiritual intensity of his subjects. The artist chose a Jew from Amsterdam to be a realistic model for Christ. But he studied his Bible carefully to guide his brushes in expressing the radiant power of love that shines through Jesus' Jewish features. Rembrandt's Christ is both the Son of Man and the Son of God, who says to us, "Take my yoke upon you, and learn from me; for I am gentle and lowly in heart, and you will find rest for your souls" (Matthew 11:29).

John C. Johnson Collection, Philadelphia

Odinokow   CHRIST AND THE SAMARITAN

*Vladimir Odinokow uses Japanese artistic tradition to interpret
Christ from an Oriental point of view. Odinokow emphasizes
Christ's identification with all mankind, regardless of the shape
of their eyes or the color of their skin, in his painting of the
Samaritan woman who met Jesus at a village well. She felt that
only in holy places could God be worshiped. But Jesus said to
her, "Woman, believe me, the hour is coming when neither
on this mountain nor in Jerusalem will you worship the Father
. . . when the true worshiper will worship the Father in spirit
and truth, for such the Father seeks to worship him"
(John 4:21-23).*

98

*Salvador Dali (1904-   ), a Spanish Roman Catholic, uses
many intriguing devices to interpret the dynamic event in the
Upper Room when Christ instituted the Sacrament of Holy
Communion. Dali designs every part of the painting—the
bowed heads of the disciples, the broken bread, the creases in
the tablecloth—to lead our eyes to Christ. Above the table
are sections of a twelve-sided geometric figure called a
dodecahedron, an ancient symbol of the universe. Christ points
upward to the form of God, who is both outside and inside
the world he has created and who has the same physical body
as Christ. This gesture reminds us of Jesus' teaching "He who
has seen me has seen the Father" (John 14:9).*

Dali   *THE SACRAMENT OF*
THE LAST SUPPER

National Gallery of Art, Washington, D. C.
(Chester Dale Collection)

Rouault **PORTRAIT OF CHRIST**

*Georges Rouault (1871-1958), a French Roman Catholic, liked
to paint religious pictures that resembled stained-glass windows.
He created his paintings more to give us a feeling of awe and
reverence than to make us see a photographic likeness. His
iridescent colors within heavy black lines serve to foster the
worshipful atmosphere of a church within our hearts. In this
painting, he confronts us with the suffering Christ, a thorn
crown mocking his kingship, as he once stood before Pilate for
judgment. Perhaps this portrait challenges us with the same
words Jesus used to challenge Pilate: "You say that I am a king.
For this I was born, and for this I have come into the world,
to bear witness to the truth. Every one who is of the truth hears
my voice" (John 18:37).*

Nolde   **THE CRUCIFIXION**

The harsh cruelty of a crucifixion, the grim reality of death, the agonizing helplessness of the mourners, the casual unconcern of the soldiers—these elements Emil Nolde weaves into a painting of intended ugliness. Nolde (1867-1956), a German Protestant, spent most of his lifetime expressing his deepest inner feelings in violent, swirling colors. Inspired by his Bible study, the artist used paint and canvas to interpret the impact of the gospel. In the midst of darkness there is light; in the midst of this brutal scene at Calvary you can see Jesus' lips partly open as though he is saying, "Father, forgive them; for they know not what they do" (Luke 23:34).

Artist Unknown **THE REDEEMER ENTHRONED**

*Thousands of tiny bits of colored glass and tile in a dedicated
artist's hands become a moving portrait of the risen Christ.
This type of art, called mosaic, has a rich lustrous beauty,
a fitting tribute to the living Lord who now in glory, his earthly
work completed, looks searchingly at his people. His left hand
holds a scepter symbolizing power and judgment, but his right
hand is raised in benediction. The compassion and affection
on his face echo his words, "Lo, I am with you always . . ."
(Matthew 28:20).*

*This sixth-century mosaic decorated a wall of the Basilica di S. Apollinare
Nuovo in Ravenna, Italy. The basilica (or church) was built in a cemetery,
over the grave of the priest Apollinaris, who was martyred for his faith.*

Part Five

Our Greatest Need

16

SINNERS NEED A SAVIOR

Problems, problems. You have problems; your friends have problems. Everybody has problems. There are problems at school, problems on the athletic field, problems at home, problems with friends. There are even problems when you are alone. Sometimes it seems that much of your time is spent trying to decide between right and wrong ways of solving your problems. Even when we know what God expects of us, it is hard to obey him. In fact, we know that we are unable to keep his Commandments by our own power. Our human nature leads us, like Adam and Eve before us, to say "no" to God's directions for holy living. That's when our problems begin. When we, for one reason or another, follow our own ways and cut God out, we get into all kinds of difficulties.

> ### TO READ AND THINK ABOUT
> Mark 7:21-23   Jesus' List of Sins
> Proverbs 6:16-19   Seven Abominations
> Proverbs 24:8-9   The Mischief-Maker
> Revelation 21:1-4, 22-27   The New Jerusalem
> Isaiah 40:1-5   Preparing the Way
> Isaiah 7:14   Immanuel
> 1 Corinthians 6:9-11   Paul's List of Sins

who is to blame?

You could blame God for all your troubles; a great many people do. It's easy to feel that if God lets you live in a world of so many problems and does nothing about it, he is responsible for all the jams you get in.

But is God really to blame for your sins? God doesn't make you selfish or hard-hearted or disobedient. He gave you the ability to choose what you want to do with your life. Think of the problems you and your friends face. Aren't wrong choices involved with every human problem? And isn't failure to love behind most wrong choices?

failure to love

Knowing right from wrong is a fairly easy attainment, largely a matter of education and experience. Anyone with a reasonable amount of intelligence can understand what God expects of him if he carefully studies God's Word. The Ten Commandments are clear

109

and precise. However, doing what is right is not easy. In fact, it is extremely difficult. The more we know about what God tells us to do, the more we see that we have failed to live by his will.

There is not one commandment that we are capable of fulfilling, especially if we remember that Jesus summarized the Commandments in terms of "You shall love . . . ." Jesus pointed out that the love of God is the starting point of keeping the Commandments. "As the Father has loved me, so have I loved you; abide in my love," he said. "If you keep my commandments, you will abide in my love, just as I have kept my Father's commandments and abide in his love" (John 15:9-10). This kind of love means complete and unconditional trust in God; it means to be open to him so that his love may flow through us to our neighbors. But no matter how hard we try to keep the Commandments, we are conscious of our lack of this kind of love. By our own power, we are incapable of loving God "with all our heart," of putting all our trust in him. No wonder, then, we find it equally impossible to love our neighbors "as ourselves." Our sinful natures get in the road of our best intentions.

the reality of sin

By now, in your experience of growing up, you do not need to be convinced about the reality of sin. You have become acquainted with many of the evil forces in the world. You know how many times you have been tempted to go against God's holy will. You know how guilty and lonely and ashamed you can feel when you are conscious of your own sinning. This is the starting place for asking God's forgiveness.

If you were ill with a serious disease, you wouldn't try to treat yourself with whatever pills happened to be in the medicine closet at home. Nor would you try to pretend that you were not sick. You would go to your doctor, recognizing the seriousness of the disease and knowing that only he could heal you.

Sin is like a sickness. It breaks our relationship with God; it forces us to face our problems alone. It leaves us weak, confused, and subject to many difficulties. Our inability to trust God fully and to love other people as God loves them becomes a spreading infection that robs us of our contentment and spoils the good that we can do with our lives. Only when we recognize the reality of sin and the fact that we are sinful people, are we capable of asking God as the great physician to heal us.

God offers help

God knows, as we do when we are honest with ourselves, that we cannot follow his will for us without his help. We need a savior, one who will help us overcome evil with good. As early as Old Testament days, God promised his people that he would send a Messiah

to earth. The word *Messiah* means "the anointed one of God."
When the Messiah came he would be the savior of the world, a
helper for everyone who accepted him.

Through the centuries before Christ was born, the Israelites believed the Messiah was coming. They didn't know when he would
come but they believed that one day he would appear. When they
wavered in their faith, there were always prophets who reminded
them of God's promise that the Lord's anointed one would deliver
them from their problems and grant them strength and power to
overcome their sins.

As you read what Jesus said and did, you realize that God cares
what happens to you and to all people. Freely he gives his Son to
be your friend and savior, seeking to help you live a satisfying and
creative life. But don't think that, through Jesus Christ, God is
giving you some kind of magical gift which will enable you to live
a perfect life or to master certain virtues. In Christ, God comes to
change you into a new person, altogether trusting in him and
altogether loving in your relationships with others. You only have
to let him live within you, to ask his renewing forgiveness daily.
To study the meaning of Jesus Christ's ministry here on earth is
to make some wonderful discoveries about the kind of person you
can become.

purifying the heart

Nathaniel Hawthorne wrote a memorable short story, called
Earth's Holocaust, which tells about a group of people who wanted
to become better persons. They piled up all their useless and silly
possessions until they had a stack as high as a mountain. Then
someone touched a match to the fire. The flames roared in a great
blazing holocaust. Some other people who did not like this sort of
thing stood around looking sad. Suddenly the Devil appeared and
told these unhappy folks to be happy. Their world of evil was not
ruined. True, the good people were trying to rid themselves of junk.
"But," said Satan, "there is one thing that these wiseacres have
forgotten."

"What is that?" the dejected ones demanded.

"Why, the human heart," replied Satan. "Unless they can hit
upon some trick of purifying that foul thing, it will soon be the same
old world again."

Hawthorne put his finger on a great truth. Unless a person can
purify himself within, he will have a hard time trying to live a holy
life. But to be purified within, man needs to have his whole life
changed, and he cannot do this for himself. God, knowing this
pressing need of mankind, sent Jesus Christ to change men, to give
them new lives. Jesus had only one mission—to bring all people
into closer fellowship with God through forgiveness of sins.

111

17

PETER'S EXPERIENCES WITH CHRIST

Have you ever wished you could have lived when Jesus lived? Then you could have seen his crude birthplace for yourself. Perhaps you could have touched an ox yoke or a dinner table that he made with primitive tools in his father's carpenter shop in Nazareth. Maybe you could have witnessed some of the miracles he performed, or heard him tell one of his parables.

TO READ AND THINK ABOUT

John 1:35-42   Becoming a Disciple
Matthew 14:22-33   Walking on Water
Luke 5:1-11   Catching Fish
Matthew 17:1-8   Transfiguration
Mark 14:32-42   Gethsemane
Luke 22:54-62   Peter's Denial
Matthew 16:13-20   Peter's Confession

No matter how hard we wish, we cannot go back to Jesus' day. But we can get a picture of what Jesus was like by seeing his impact on someone who knew him well. Take Peter, for instance. Through Peter's experiences, you can get a good idea of what it was like to live when Jesus was here on earth.

Despite his glaring faults, Peter was a likable person. In his fumbling, stumbling way he managed to grow in his understanding of his relationship with God through Christ. Many people pick Peter as their favorite disciple. Perhaps they see some of their own strengths and weaknesses in him. Perhaps they feel that if Christ could forgive him, if Christ could help him conquer his doubts correct his stupid blunders, and solve his problems, there is hope for them, too. Peter is a vivid example of a sinful man conscious of his need of a savior.

"the big fisherman"

There are many things we do not know about Peter. We don't know how old he was or what he looked like. Legend describes him as a big man, a rough, burly individualist.

Probably Peter (at first known as Simon) was a fisherman on the lake, in partnership with his brother Andrew and his friends James and John, the sons of Zebedee. Working out-of-doors in all kinds of weather, these men were toughened to hardships and skilled in handling difficulties. Their skin bronzed by sun and wind, their hands callused from straining at their oars and hauling in nets, Galilean fishermen were a hardy breed. There is no doubt that Peter and his partners were rugged, independent men, accustomed to being self-reliant. If they gave their loyalty to a cause or to a man, they did so because they believed it was the right decision to make. The fact that these fishermen were among the first disciples called by Jesus is significant. He excited them with his invitation to join him, to become fishers of men. They accepted the challenge.

Actually, Andrew was the first of the group to give his loyalty to Jesus. Andrew had been going regularly to the banks of the River Jordan to listen to the fiery sermons of John the Baptist. He may even have become one of John's disciples. But on the day John pointed out Jesus to the crowds, saying, "Behold, the Lamb of God, who takes away the sin of the world," Andrew knew that this carpenter from Nazareth was the man he must follow.

Rushing home, Andrew found Peter at his nets. Bursting with enthusiasm, Andrew shouted, "We have found the Messiah!" (*Christ* is a Greek word meaning Messiah). Peter was impressed. Without a word he let his brother take him to Jesus. He, too, became a disciple.

a disciple learns

Peter quickly became a close friend of Jesus. He took the Lord into his home and entertained him. Once, when he was there, Jesus healed Peter's mother-in-law, who was seriously ill. Obviously, then, Peter was married. But whether his wife was dead when he became a disciple or whether he left her behind when he went to follow Jesus, we don't know. The Gospels tell us very little about the personal lives of those who gave up so much to follow Jesus.

Peter went wherever Jesus went. He heard the Lord teach the multitudes that swarmed around him; he sat quietly, trying to absorb Christ's words about the loving fatherhood of God and the consequent brotherhood of man. Many of the teachings reported in the four Gospels were directed specifically to Peter and the other disciples, preparing them to take over Christ's earthly ministry when he would be gone from their midst. It must have been difficult for a man who had spent most of his life at physical labor, and who had had little time for thinking or meditating, to understand all the great spiritual truths Jesus emphasized.

Most of the miracles Peter witnessed were really acted-out

113

parables, for Jesus often dramatized his teachings. Peter found these particularly hard to grasp. One night, when he and the others were sitting in a boat out on the lake, they saw Jesus walking toward them on the water. They were frightened; he looked like a ghost. But when Jesus spoke and reassured them, they became calm. Immediately, Peter wanted to walk on the water, too. "Lord, if it is you, bid me come to you on the water," he called. "Come," said Jesus. Peter climbed out of the boat and started walking. But the high winds scared him, and because he was afraid, because his trust in Jesus' protection was not strong enough, he sank into the waves. Christ rescued him and put him back in the boat. "O man of little faith, why did you doubt?" Jesus asked gently (Matthew 14:28-33). Peter had not understood that Jesus was trying to show him how trust in God would sustain and protect him.

Another time Peter had been fishing all night with James and John. They had caught nothing. Tired and frustrated, they returned to the shore. There they saw Jesus teaching a group of people by the lake. As Jesus finished speaking, he saw the downcast disciples and told them to go fishing again. This time he ordered them to go out where the water was very deep. The disciples did so, and when they pulled in their nets, the nets were filled with fish—so many fish that the boats began to sink. When they had brought the catch back to shore, Peter went to Jesus and fell down at his feet, saying, "Depart from me, for I am a sinful man, O Lord."

Peter must have felt very guilty because he had doubted Christ's wisdom in sending him back to the lake after he had fished so long and so unsuccessfully. Once more, his trust in Jesus had not been strong enough. But Jesus told Peter not to be afraid. "Henceforth you will be catching men," he added (Luke 5:1-11).

what peter thought of Christ

One day Jesus and his disciples were traveling through the city of Caesarea Philippi on their way to the Mount of Transfiguration. As they walked along the dusty roads, Jesus questioned his companions about the reactions of people who heard him speak and saw his miracles. "Who do men say that the Son of man is?" he asked.

The disciples answered frankly. Some people thought he was John the Baptist. Others believed he was Elijah, or the prophet Jeremiah, come back to earth. Jesus looked around at his twelve followers: "But who do you say that I am?"

Peter acted as spokesman for the group. Slowly, meaningfully, he replied, "You are the Christ, the Son of the living God." Jesus was pleased with the depth of Peter's understanding, and said to him: "Blessed are you, Simon the son of Jonah! For flesh and blood has not revealed this to you, but my Father who is in heaven. And I tell you, you are Peter, and on this rock I will build my church, and the powers of death shall not prevail against it" (Matthew 16:13-18). Probably, up to this time, everyone had called Peter by his real name, Simon. Now Jesus had given him a new name, the name by which we remember him. He had called him Peter, which means "the rock." It was Peter's confession of Jesus as the Messiah that prompted Jesus to call him "the rock." Jesus made it very clear that his church is built on the solid rock of those who confess their faith in him as their Lord.

a disciple fails

Understanding truth is one thing; living by it is quite another. Peter was keen enough to sense that Jesus was the savior God had sent to his people, but he had a hard time letting the full impact of this truth guide his words and actions. In this respect he wasn't much different from us.

While Jesus and his disciples were making their way through the north of Palestine one day, Jesus talked about the future. He told his disciples that soon many evil things would happen to him. In Jerusalem, he said, he would suffer and be killed. But on the third day, he added, he would rise again. Peter didn't like this talk about death. He couldn't grasp the fact that a messiah might willingly

suffer at the hands of those who rejected him. He couldn't see any sense in Jesus going on to Jerusalem if danger lurked there. "God forbid, Lord!" he exploded. "This shall never happen to you."

"Get behind me, Satan!" Jesus answered. "You are a hindrance to me; for you are not on the side of God, but of men" (Matthew 16:21-23). Very bluntly, Jesus tried to make Peter realize that, in objecting to his death and resurrection, Peter was really serving Satan rather than God. Though Peter wanted to protect Jesus, he was standing in the way of Jesus' doing what God had planned.

Immediately after this incident, Jesus took Peter, James, and John with him to the Mount of Transfiguration. There, on that high mountain peak, Peter had an awesome experience. A dazzling radiance surrounded Christ and the voice of God said, "This is my beloved Son . . . ." Moses, the great lawgiver, and the prophet Elijah appeared with Jesus. Peter's enthusiasm knew no limits. He said to Jesus, "Lord, it is well that we are here; if you wish, I will make three booths here, one for you and one for Moses and one for Elijah" (Matthew 17:1-8). He wanted to stay on the mountaintop and forget about the rest of the world. If he could build some cabins there for these great religious leaders, he could remain close to them for the rest of his life. Kindly, Jesus declined his offer and led his disciples back down the mountainside to the plain where a distraught father had brought his epileptic son to be healed. Peter had a hard time understanding that Jesus had to return from the mountaintop if he were to help people in need.

This impetuous Peter, who wanted to protect his Lord from any harm and isolate him on a mountaintop, fell asleep in the Garden of Gethsemane when he could have been of real service. Here Jesus came to pray after he had shared his sacramental Last Supper with his disciples in the Upper Room of a Jerusalem home. Knowing that the time of his death was near, Jesus took Peter, James, and John with him into the Garden to share his last moments of devotion. But Peter and the others couldn't keep awake. Here was an opportunity for Peter to shield Jesus from harm while he prayed, and instead the disciple was stretched out on the ground in slumber. Jesus was keenly disappointed.

Earlier in the day, Peter had boasted, "Lord, I am ready to go with you to prison and to death." Jesus had replied, "I tell you, Peter, the cock will not crow this day, until you three times deny that you know me" (Luke 22:33-34). Peter had failed Jesus in his hour of prayer. Would he deny him, too?

That night, at the edge of the Garden, Jesus was arrested. Peter rose from his slumbers to defend his master. Swinging his sword, he cut off the ear of Malchus, a servant of the high priest. Peter thought he was doing the right thing. Jesus disagreed, ". . . All who take the sword will perish by the sword." To make his point more vivid, Jesus healed the wounded servant (Luke 22:50-51).

When Jesus was taken to the court of the high priest in Jerusalem, Peter followed cautiously at a distance. Later he entered the courtyard to see what would happen to Jesus. Seeing Peter sitting by a fire, a maid told the people standing around that Peter was with Jesus when he was arrested. "Woman," Peter insisted, "I do not know him." A little later a man accused Peter of being a follower of Jesus: "You also are one of them." Peter denied the charge hotly, saying, "Man, I am not." Still later another man accused him of being with Jesus in the province of Galilee. Again Peter denied even knowing Jesus: "Man, I do not know what you are saying."

At that moment a rooster crowed; dawn was breaking. Peter looked up and caught the saddened eyes of Jesus. He left the courtyard and wept. He had failed as a disciple (Luke 22:54-62).

peter carries on

The time came, after Christ's death and resurrection, when Peter was challenged again to remember his confession of faith and his call to discipleship. Now, however, he saw things in a clearer light. He had been to the empty tomb. He knew he was forgiven and that Christ, his risen Lord, still wanted him to carry on his work as a disciple. Even though he would continue to fail time after time, he knew that Christ's daily forgiveness would restore his trust in God.

As a leader of the early church in Jerusalem, the big fisherman was constantly busy—preaching, teaching, doing whatever he could to unify this fledgling congregation. The coming of the Holy Spirit at Pentecost not only brought the church into being, but also helped Christians like Peter understand the power of Jesus more fully. One day, by the gate to the Temple, Peter—by Christ's power—healed a man who had been lame from birth. Great crowds swarmed around him to see this miracle. Peter preached to them about Jesus, saying, "And his name, by faith in his name, has made this man strong whom you see and know . . ." (Acts 3:16).

While he and John were preaching, the priests heard them and had them arrested. The next day, they were brought before the Sanhedrin (the Jewish court presided over by the high priest). This was the same group of Jewish rulers, elders, and scribes who had condemned Jesus. While Peter knew that once again his life was in danger, this time he did not deny his Lord. When the court charged him to stop speaking and teaching in the name of Jesus, Peter squared his shoulders and replied, "Whether it is right in the sight of God to listen to you rather than to God, you must judge; for we cannot but speak of what we have seen and heard" (Acts 4:1-20). The forgiven "man of rock" was now, with God's help, doing a better job of living up to his name.

Part Six

Jesus Christ Is My Lord

18

JESUS CHRIST IS TRUE GOD

If we are to accept Christ as our Lord, then we need to know who he is and why he has a right to claim lordship over us. It is helpful for us to read about the experiences of men like Peter who lived very close to Christ. It is also good to study the beliefs of those early followers of Christ who composed statements of the faith, which we call creeds. Carefully and concisely, they expressed basic truths that we should know and believe about Christ.

> TO READ AND THINK ABOUT
> *John 1:1-14   The Word Became Flesh*
> *Matthew 3:13-17   Jesus' Baptism*
> *Matthew 17:1-8   The Transfiguration*
> *John 3:16-21   God So Loved*
> *John 10:22-30   I and the Father Are One*
> *John 14:8-11   I Am in the Father*
> *John 17:1-5   Jesus in Prayer*

the church and its creeds

As the church began spreading from Jerusalem to other cities, some of the church missionary leaders, such as Paul, began to write letters interpreting the Christian faith for the fledgling congregations. Some of these letters (called "epistles" in Greek) were written to answer specific doubts and problems; others explained the important teachings of Christianity. Later, Gospel stories of the life of Christ were prepared and circulated among the churches for the benefit of those who did not know the details of Christ's life on earth. New Christians, scattered all over the Mediterranean world, wanted to learn all they could about Christ. Eventually, these writings were collected into one volume, which we call the New Testament.

During this period, and for the next three hundred years, the church worked hard to develop creeds—simple, yet clear, statements of the Christian faith which would help people remember the essential beliefs. The word "creed" comes from the Latin *credo*, meaning "I believe." The earliest Christian creeds were probably statements like "I believe that Jesus is Lord," or to use Peter's words, "I believe that Jesus is 'the Christ, the Son of the living God.'" Over the century that followed, creeds became more complex.

You are already familiar with two creeds used in The Service. The Nicene Creed is used especially at services of Holy Communion and on festive days. The Apostles' Creed is used more frequently. We usually confess our faith using the Apostles' Creed immediately following the reading of the Gospel lesson on Sunday morning. It is also used as part of the baptismal and confirmation services. These two creeds have come down to us from the early centuries of the church's existence.

an unbroken line

Thanks to those who forged the Apostles' and Nicene Creeds, Christianity has remembered its basic faith. Each new generation of Christians using these words as their own has helped keep the faith intact through the centuries. Of course, the church and its teachings have often been under attack. And, many times, Christians have weakened in their faith. But there has always been a nucleus of dedicated Christians who were willing to live and die for the truth that Jesus Christ was their Lord.

The early church has left us, as a legacy, the combined privilege and responsibility of making its treasured creeds our own. With that long, unbroken line of witnesses stretching back to the first congregation in an upper room in Jerusalem, we join in saying, "I believe . . . in Jesus Christ his only Son our Lord." This is very important to our faith. It means that we base our willingness to follow Christ on the fact that through him we come to know God.

the unveiling of God

Have you ever attended the unveiling of a new work of art? As you arrived, you noticed that the art piece was covered with a cloth. Maybe you had some idea what the work of art was like, or at least what its subject was. You probably let your imagination create a picture, but you could not be sure how accurate your picture was. Then came the moment of unveiling. The cloth was taken off, and you saw the work of art for the first time.

Men have always had some ideas about God. But God was veiled; he wasn't seen. Pagans usually confused the creator with the things he created. Therefore, they worshiped the sun, or stars, or rocks, or fire or else they made idols to worship. One reason they made idols was because they wanted to see God.

In Old Testament times, God revealed his will through those who spoke for him. Prophets and other leaders repeated God's words but they couldn't show God himself. He was still veiled. But when you turn to the New Testament, it is like tearing aside a veil. In Jesus, God revealed himself. Now every man, by knowing Jesus, could come to know God.

knowing God in Christ

Jesus not only tells us about his Father but, by his own example, shows us how God acts. In Jesus, we see God's compassion for the outcasts of society, for people in need, for people with problems. We come to realize that God really cares what happens to every person. As he deals with his people, he is kind and gentle, always treating them with thoughtfulness, always treating them according to their individual needs. Jesus treated the bombastic, headstrong Peter differently than he did the quiet John or the doubting Thomas or the confused Philip. He told one rich man to sell all his goods and give the proceeds to the poor; he told another rich man to prepare his home for a visit. Though both men were wealthy, Jesus treated each one according to his greatest need. So God works with his people, helping each one to become the kind of person God would have him be.

Jesus frequently taught in parables, forcing men to think through them and interpret them. He wanted people to think for themselves,

121

to choose God's way of life because they loved and trusted God, because they were thankful for his many blessings. God doesn't want us to be puppets dangling from the ends of strings. He wants our loyalty and devotion because we choose to dedicate ourselves to him.

Knowing God in Jesus Christ is different from knowing God in any other way. There are many religions in the world which confess faith in God. Only Christianity professes knowledge of God through Jesus Christ and accepts the fact that Jesus Christ is the Son of God. All other religions have to try and figure out what God is like without this firsthand experience of him. Christians do not have to seek God. He comes to them in Jesus Christ and gives himself and his love to all who will receive Christ as Lord.

Christ is eternal

In his explanation of the Second Article of the Apostles' Creed, Luther wrote, "I believe that Jesus Christ—true God, Son of the Father from eternity, . . . is my Lord." The phrase "from eternity" is important. Christ did not begin his life on that first Christmas. As the second person of the Trinity, Christ was always with the Father. Read the words of the Nicene Creed carefully. He is described as "begotten of his Father before all worlds," as "being of one substance with the Father, By whom all things were made. . . ." In the first chapter of his Gospel, John speaks of Christ as the incarnate (in human form) Word of God. "In the beginning was the Word, and the Word was with God, and the Word was God . . . And the Word became flesh and dwelt among us, full of grace and truth; we have beheld his glory, glory as of the only Son from the Father" (John 1:1, 14). Does this discussion of Christ as eternal sound confusing to you? To say that he has always been in existence and will always be in existence is another way of saying that Jesus the Christ is God. He is not a half-God. He is not someone like God. He is not just a worker of miracles or a teller of stories. He is divine. He is one with God.

19

JESUS CHRIST IS TRUE MAN

There's an old story about a man who was taking a walk through a pasture. He came upon an anthill and amused himself by watching the ants as they busily scurried in and out. Then he happened to move into a position which cast his shadow over the anthill. Immediately all activity ceased. The ants disappeared into their home. When he stepped back so that his shadow was not over the anthill, the ants resumed their activities.

> ### TO READ AND THINK ABOUT
> *Luke 2:1-20   The Christmas Story*
> *Matthew 1:18-25   As Joseph Told It*
> *Matthew 2:1-12   Visit of the Wise Men*
> *Matthew 8:23-27   "What Sort of Man?"*
> *1 Timothy 2:5-6   The Man*
> *Hebrews 2:10-18   He Is Able to Help*
> *Hebrews 4:14-16   As We Are*

Intrigued by the ants' reaction to shadow and light, he proceeded to conduct a little experiment. Again he let his shadow fall on the hill. The ants disappeared. Then he moved away. Once more the ants became busy as soon as his shadow was gone. Evidently, they were afraid of the sudden darkness.

The man wondered how he could prove to the ants that he meant them no harm. He finally concluded that the only way he could do this successfully would be to become an ant himself. Then he could communicate with the ants; he could convince them that he wanted to be their friend. Of course, no man can become an ant— but God can become a man, and that is what he did.

God is concerned about his people. He created and loves them; he wants to help them. But men turn against God and insist on their own sinful ways. Because they have done this, they are afraid of God and of the punishment they justly deserve for their sins. Like the scurrying ants who were afraid of the man, men don't understand that God wants to help them, not hurt them. It was in order to overcome the barriers between God and men, and enable them to know him, that he became a man in Jesus Christ. We express our belief in his having become a man when we repeat the creedal statements that he was born to Mary, that he suffered, that he was crucified, and that he died.

the incarnation

God's coming to man in Jesus is called the Incarnation. The word "incarnation" comes from the Latin which means "in the body." It wasn't that God just looked like a man; he actually became a man.

Christmas is the day on which we celebrate the birth of Jesus to Mary at Bethlehem. Here in a crude stable near an inn the mystery of the Incarnation took place. To demonstrate the completeness of his humanity, God chose to be born of a human mother in the natural process whereby every person enters the world.

Just as you were once a helpless baby unable to talk or walk, so was Jesus. He was dependent upon Mary and Joseph for his care, for food and clothing, for all that he needed. When his life was in danger because of the murderous anger of King Herod, his family escaped from the country to take him to Egypt and safety.

Jesus grew slowly, as a child grows. He probably learned to take his first step in the hot sands of Egypt; he spoke his first words there, too. Later, when Joseph had taken Mary and Jesus to make their home in Nazareth, we can imagine Jesus developing into a normal, happy boy. Certainly he played games with his friends around the village well and on the rocky hillsides, filled with caves and crevices to explore. His life was full of all the rich experiences of boyhood.

In his home there were younger brothers and sisters. He had four brothers, James, Joses, Judas, and Simon. But, although he had sisters, their names aren't mentioned in the New Testament nor are we told how many there were. It was a big family. Jesus was probably never lonely.

Since he was the oldest boy, it was natural that he should help Joseph in the carpentry shop. As the years went by, he learned to fashion farming tools, to build doors for houses, and to fix wooden toys for the village children. It may be that Joseph died while Jesus was still a youth and he had to use his woodworking skills to support the family. There is no doubt that Jesus knew the back-breaking toil of honest work and the sweetness of rest at the end of the day.

He learned about God from his parents and from the rabbis in the synagogue. In boyhood he must have gone to school; all Jewish boys did. When he was twelve, he went with his parents at Passover time to the Temple in Jerusalem. He took advantage of the situation by spending most of his time there asking the rabbis questions. He was eager to learn. According to custom, Jewish boys were considered adults at the age of twelve. Jesus' boyhood was over. It is significant that his manhood began in the Temple.

The next eighteen years are shrouded in mystery. We can only guess that Jesus continued to work as a carpenter, preparing himself for the great day to come.

When he was thirty years old, Jesus entered his special ministry, a ministry marked by at least three years of preaching, teaching, and healing. The Four Gospels give us many insights into his human nature during his public ministry. All men are subject to temptations; Jesus was tempted, too. But he did not give in to evil. At Jacob's well in Samaria, Jesus asked for water to drink. He grew thirsty as any man does, and hungry as well. He knew what it was to be weary, lonely, and disappointed. Before Lazarus' tomb, he wept in sorrow as a man weeps at the loss of a close friend. In the Garden of Gethsemane and on Good Friday, he knew physical and mental agony. There was no play-acting on the cross. Jesus suffered terrible pain as the nails tore at his flesh and the crown of thorns sent little rivulets of blood down his face. When the soldiers offered him wine mixed with a drug to lessen the pain, Jesus refused to drink. He didn't want to lose control of his senses; there was so little time left. When he died finally, as all men must die, many of those in the jeering crowd praised his manly conduct in his agony.

a real man

Just as Jesus Christ is "true God," said Luther, he is also "true man." Don't think of Jesus as some kind of superman. He wasn't. If he had been, the revelation of God would never have seemed real. He still would have been above us, unaware of the problems we face, the worries and tensions we feel.

How could Jesus be God and man at the same time? This is a question many have tried to answer. The writers of the New Testament and the creed builders are content to tell us that Jesus is truly God and that he is truly man; they make no attempt to explain how he could be both at the same time. Perhaps they feel it isn't really important that we know *how* Jesus is both God and man simultaneously. Maybe we don't have the mental capacity to understand this mystery anyway.

There is an old fable about a remarkable scholar, a very brilliant man, who insisted he could only believe those portions of the Bible that he could explain logically. One day, by the seashore, the scholar saw an angel trying to empty all the water of the sea into a small seashell. This sight struck him as funny, and he laughed out loud. "Don't laugh," said the angel. "It is no more foolish for me to try and empty the water of the sea into this seashell than it is for you to try and limit the unlimited God by your limited mind."

To be able to explain *how* Jesus could be God and man isn't so important as to understand *why* God chose this method of revealing himself. By truly being man, Jesus could identify himself with people. He could know by experience the joys and sorrows of life; he could see life from man's point of view. Further, he could demonstrate the perfect kind of human life, with complete trust in God and complete love for his fellowmen, that the heavenly Father intends everyone to live. By also being fully God, Jesus could take man's sin on himself and destroy it.

one with us

We have no authentic pictures of Jesus. As far as we know, no one in his day painted his portrait. The Jews, of course, believed that this would be breaking the First Commandment. Through the years, many artists of different nationalities have tried their skill in portraying Jesus. Many of the great Middle Age and Renaissance paintings of Christ show Jesus as an Italian simply because most of the artists and their models were Italian. In the paintings of Northern Europe, Jesus looks Dutch or German or Scandinavian. In the Orient, you can see pictures of Jesus which show him as Chinese, Japanese, or Indian. In Africa, there are paintings which portray him as a Negro. Why not? Although he was a Jew of the house and lineage of David, Jesus came to all men everywhere to be their personal Savior and Lord. Of course, we could insist that art must be historically accurate, that Jesus should be shown with Jewish features and with the clothing of his day. But isn't the magnificent fact about the power of Christ simply that he cannot be imprisoned in history or in any part of the world? We don't have to go back 2,000 years to Jerusalem to find him. He comes to Honolulu, Calgary, San Juan, and Albuquerque to find us.

In the nineteenth century, a Roman Catholic priest named Damien went out to Hawaii, to work in the leper colony on the island of Molokai. For years, Father Damien labored among the sufferers of the dread disease. He was greatly admired and respected. But never was he able to get close to his parishioners and really help them—not until one Sunday when he entered his pulpit and began his sermon with the words "We lepers." He had physically become one with his people. Now they knew how great his love for them was.

This is what Jesus has done for us. He has physically identified himself with every human being—with you. He has brought God into the world and made him someone you know, someone you can love and trust. God is no longer a stranger. In Jesus, you know for sure that God belongs to you and you belong to him.

20

IMPORTANT DAYS IN JESUS' LIFE

There are a number of important days in your life. The day of your birth is one. The day you were baptized is another. Confirmation day will be one. This will be followed in a few years by high-school graduation day.

TO READ AND THINK ABOUT
Matthew 21:1-11   Triumphal Entry
Luke 22:7-23   In the Upper Room
Matthew 26:36-56   Gethsemane
Matthew 26:57-75   Before Caiaphas; Peter's Denial
Mark 15:1-15   Before Pilate
Mark 15:16-39   The Crucifixion
John 20:1-18   He Is Risen

There were important days in the life of Jesus while he was on earth. We usually observe these days in our church worship each year. These days remind us of Christ's godhood and manhood, of how he helps us become united with God.

great days

One of these days is Christmas, which the church celebrates as the day when Jesus was born. Another is Epiphany Day (January 6), when the wise men visited Jesus. Since they were Gentiles, their pilgrimage to the manger reminds us that Jesus belongs to all men.

There is Transfiguration Day (in August) when Jesus received his Father's blessings. You remember how Moses and Elijah appeared on the mountaintop with him, symbolizing the fact that his ministry was fulfilling the Law and the teachings of the Old Testament prophets. In a certain sense, the transfiguration of Jesus was also an epiphany day, a day when Jesus revealed the divine glory of God in his own body.

There is Palm Sunday, when Jesus entered the city of Jerusalem to the cheers of the crowds thronging the streets to acclaim their King. There is Maundy Thursday, the day on which Jesus instituted the Sacrament of Holy Communion. There is Good Friday, when he died on the cross. And there is Easter, when he arose triumphantly from the dead.

Christians also remember Ascension Day. He who had come from the Father at Christmas now shares glory with the Father throughout eternity but is ever near to those who need him and accept him.

Although Pentecost (also called Whitsunday) is not strictly a day in the life of Christ, we remember it because the Christian church was born on this day. Just as Jesus had promised, the Holy Spirit was poured out upon the disciples in Jerusalem.

Each of these days which you celebrate in the church yearly is important. We need to observe them all in our thinking, study, and worship. Christmas without Easter would leave the world with a God who had no power over death. Easter without Pentecost would demonstrate God's victory over death, but would suggest that God forgot his people still needed the presence of the Holy Spirit.

the significance of holy week

Of all the events in the life of Christ, those which took place in the last week of his life are the ones the church has singled out as the most meaningful. The Apostles' Creed, for instance, says that Jesus was "conceived by the Holy Ghost, Born of the Virgin Mary," and then immediately adds, "Suffered under Pontius Pilate, Was crucified, dead and buried . . . The third day he rose again from the dead . . . ." Nothing is mentioned in the creeds about any of his teachings or any of his miracles. The decisive thing that Jesus did, according to the early Christians, was to rise from the dead after giving his life on the cross.

The whole of Christ's life points to this one particular week. He knew it was coming. Willingly, he let the trials and tortures of this week take place. Several times, he had predicted to his disciples that he would be put to death by those who hated him. He had also told them that, although this would happen, on the third day he would rise again. They, of course, didn't understand what he was saying.

This last week, from Palm Sunday to Easter Sunday, the church calls "Holy Week." During these days, you have a special opportunity to remember that God is holy and that, in his holiness, he invites you to be holy, too. This could never have happened without Christ's ministry to you. If there were no Holy Week, you would always be separated from God rather than united with him in love.

Think of what happened in Holy Week. All Four Gospels give us rich details of those eventful days. On Palm Sunday, Jesus entered Jerusalem to the shouted "Hosannas" of the crowds who came to see him. He was announcing himself publicly as God's Messiah. But he was riding a donkey, the symbol of peace. Many in the multitudes were disturbed. They expected the Messiah, if he were truly of the line of David, to be riding a war horse. Surely the Messiah would raise the flag of revolt and lead his people to military victory over the hated Roman conquerors. But Jesus had no intention of stirring up armed revolt. He wanted men to carry on inward revolutions, turning against their own sinfulness. In just five days, many of those who enthusiastically welcomed Jesus would be shouting, "Crucify him!" But today, everyone waited to see what he would do next.

Some were startled when he strode angrily into the Temple the next day and proceeded to drive out the money-changers and the livestock peddlers. After all, exchanging foreign currency for Jewish coins and providing spotless, well-bred animals for sacrifices was considered a legitimate business. What right did Jesus have to take the responsibility of changing things? He made more enemies that day when he said, "Is it not written, 'My house shall be called a house of prayer for all the nations'? But you have made it a den of robbers" (Mark 11:17).

In the days that followed, various influential Jewish groups, like the Pharisees and the Sadducees, kept deliberately getting Jesus into arguments, hoping to trick him into saying something heretical, something damaging to their doctrines of God. The number of his enemies grew, and even the high priest was searching for ways to get rid of this carpenter from Nazareth who claimed he was God's Anointed One.

Jesus wanted to tell all men about the heavenly Father who loved them. But the great crowds who followed him during the early part of the week were thinning out. The clouds of opposition were growing thicker, blacker. Swiftly, the week was moving to its climax. Even now, one of his own disciples was plotting to betray him.

maundy thursday

On Thursday, at sundown, Jesus took his disciples to the Upper Room to celebrate the Passover meal with them. At Passover time, every devout Jew remembered the bitterness of his ancestors when they were held captive in Egypt. And they remembered the goodness of God, who sent Moses to free them from bondage and lead them through the wilderness to the Promised Land. As Jesus sat there with this small, devoted band of men, who had been with him through the many experiences of his ministry, he knew that soon his life on earth would be over. Judas had made all the arrangements to betray him to his enemies. Slowly he took the bread from the table and, as a good host, broke it to share with his companions. But he said to them as he passed it around the table, "Take, eat; this is my body." Taking the cup of wine and blessing it with prayer, Jesus passed it to the disciples. "Drink of it, all of you," he said, "for this is my blood of the new covenant . . ." (Matthew 26: 26-28). A new covenant with God, a new testament, was taking shape—a covenant built on love and faith. By the sacrifice of his own life, Jesus was sealing this covenant.

Through the centuries that have followed, the Sacrament of Holy Communion has been a precious worship experience for Christians. As they come to the altar to receive bread and wine, they realize that God is uniting them with the living presence of his Son. They remember how Christ died on a cross, how he rose again from the dead as the living Lord, and how he offers forgiveness of sins and strength for holy living to all who will accept these great gifts. Soon you, too, will be joining the great company of Christians who come regularly to their churches to participate in the sacrament.

good friday

Friday of Holy Week was both the tragic day of Jesus' death and the thrilling day of his sacrifice. For a while men called this day "God's Friday." In time these words were misunderstood to be "Good Friday," and that name has stuck. This was the day when the new covenant was dramatically made clear to men of faith. On a lonely windswept hill outside the city walls of Jerusalem, Jesus died, forgiving his enemies. Crucified between two political revolutionaries who were being punished for their crimes against Rome, Jesus suffered painfully. In his last moments he spoke again of his complete trust in God.

We are apt to look back at that fateful day and get very angry with those who treated Jesus so vilely. Could it happen today? Suppose Jesus appeared in your community and began confronting people with God's demand for holiness. Do you think he would make enemies who would want to get rid of him, to put him to death? How about you? Would you be in the crowd shouting, "Crucify him"? Think of the words of a famous Good Friday hymn:

> Who was the guilty? Who brought this upon thee?
> Alas, my treason, Jesus, hath undone thee.
> 'Twas I, Lord Jesus, I it was denied thee:
> I crucified thee. (*SBH* 85)

easter sunday

The climax of Holy Week was not Good Friday. It was Easter. On this first day of the week, Jesus kept his promise. God raised him from the dead. The women who came to the tomb early that morning, planning to anoint his body with sweet-smelling oils, were astonished. So were his disciples when they heard the electrifying news. It was incredible. No one had really believed that Jesus would come back from the dead. But he did; he had passed through death and returned to life. The Resurrection offers vivid proof of the power of God in Christ. And God promised that whoever believed in Christ would have the same experience of eternity.

The phrase in the Apostles' Creed, "He descended into hell," is simply a statement that Jesus really died. The word "hell" was used by the creed builders to refer to a place where those who died went immediately after death. In one of his letters, Peter refers to this idea when he says that this descent into the realm of the dead was Christ's opportunity to preach the gospel, the good news, to those who had by accident of time died before his coming. "For Christ also died for sins once for all, the righteous for the unrighteous, that he might bring us to God, being put to death in the flesh but made alive in the spirit; in which he went and preached to the spirits in prison . . ." (1 Peter 3:18-19). God has ways of reaching people wherever they are.

Because of Easter, we can see the events of Holy Week—and indeed of Christ's whole life—in their proper perspective. God became Jesus so that he could live with men as a man, even die for them, and show them that they are meant to live with him forever. So great is this gift of eternal life which Jesus Christ won for us that we celebrate Easter in our churches every Sunday. The very fact that Christians changed their principal day of worship from the seventh day of the week to the first day testifies to the importance of Easter in our faith.

21

CHRIST, THE SAVIOR OF THE WORLD

An angelic song rang out one starry night to shepherds huddled around their fires on the plains of Bethlehem. Christ, the Savior, is born! You have heard this word Savior many times when people speak about Jesus. Somehow, you know it is connected with what happened at the cross and in the garden tomb of Joseph of Arimathea. To complicate the matter, both the New Testament and the church insist that Jesus is your personal Savior—if you accept him as your Lord. But what does this really mean to you?

> ### TO READ AND THINK ABOUT
> *1 Peter 3:18-20   "To the Spirits in Prison"*
> *Hebrews 10:11-31   The New and Living Way*
> *1 John 1:5-10   "If We Confess"*
> *Isaiah 53   The Suffering Servant*
> *Colossians 2:13-15   "God Made Alive"*
> *John 8:31-36   Made Free*
> *1 Peter 1:3-5, 17-21   A Living Hope*

predicaments

Suppose, one winter day when the pond was covered with a gleaming sheet of fresh ice, you wanted to go ice-skating. Your father warned you not to go because the ice was not thick enough. Yet, feeling that you knew better than he did whether or not the ice was safe, you went anyway. You wanted to go, and besides, you were a good skater; you could take care of yourself. Soon you were gliding smoothly out on the pond, your blades flashing in the sun.

Everything was fine until that first ominous crack. Another crack —a moment of hesitation—more cracks! Suddenly the ice gave way, and you found yourself plummeting into the bitterly cold water. The weight of your skates dragged you down. You called for help as you struggled to pull yourself out. But your hands kept slipping on the wet ice; your voice cracked with the cold. You felt panicky. Then you saw your father inching his way out on the ice pushing a long wooden plank before him. Slowly he brought it to your fingertips where you could grab hold. Then, carefully, he pulled you to safety. When he got you back to the bank, he put some of his own clothes around you and built a roaring fire. All the time he was working on you to restore circulation to your almost frozen body, he kept telling you how much he loved you. How would you feel? Ashamed of your disobedience? Embarrassed because you had thought you were right and he was wrong? Eager to tell him how sorry you were and how much you loved him, too? Of course! You needed a savior and miraculously one appeared just in time. Thankfulness and love welled up in you.

In much the same way, in our lives, we get ourselves into all kinds of predicaments. Our own sinful ways lead us to ignore the will and the warnings of God. The heavenly Father knows that, unless we have help, we are heading for all kinds of trouble and tragedy. That is why he sent his own Son to save us. He never stops offering his help. Even if we "fall through the ice," he is there reaching out for us.

Let's go back to our ice-skating parable. Suppose your father had drowned while saving you. For the rest of your life, you would never have been able to forget that he had died so you could live. This is the impact of the cross; Jesus gave his life for us.

the atonement

For a long time, the church did not try to explain how Christ saved men; it was content just to proclaim the good news that he did.

But men wanted to know the *how* of God's remarkable action on our behalf. They asked for logical explanations—explanations that they could understand. The church accordingly tried to find answers. Great theologians put their minds to the task. They spoke of the death and resurrection of Christ as the "atonement," the "at-one-ment" whereby Christ brought men and God together as one.

Paul and other New Testament writers tried to find ways of expressing the work of Christ in terms their readers could understand. They used a number of illustrations to describe this process of salvation. None of these illustrations is perfect; all leave some questions unanswered. What God did is far beyond the ability of men to explain or comprehend completely. We want to look carefully at some of these illustrations, however, because they are helpful in probing the meaning of words like atonement and savior.

Christ, the victor

One of the word-pictures used by the church is that of Christ, the victor over all the evil forces in the world—the victor over sin, death, and the Devil. Salvation is described in terms of Jesus' dramatic victory in his conflict with evil powers. Many times he was tempted to conduct his ministry according to worldly ways. Remember how, in the wilderness, Satan suggested he turn stones into bread, so that people would flock to his side to be fed?

Time after time, Jesus won out against temptation, even the hard temptation in the Garden of Gethsemane. There, on his knees in prayer, he asked if he could avoid all the suffering that lay before him. His human nature was rebelling at the thought of pain and death. But again he won. "My Father, if it be possible, let this cup pass from me; nevertheless, not as I will, but as thou wilt" (Matthew 26:39).

The victorious Christ leads the way to holiness in triumph. He has won the decisive victory over sin, death, and the Devil for all time. Therefore, we choose him as our champion. Paul reflected this idea when he wrote, "Who shall separate us from the love of Christ? Shall tribulation, or distress, or persecution, or famine, or nakedness, or peril, or sword? . . . No, in all these things we are more than conquerors through him who loved us" (Romans 8:35, 37). Our faith in Christ, our trust in him, is all we need to join the winning side. John pointed out, "For whatever is born of God overcomes the world; and this is the victory that overcomes the world, our faith" (1 John 5:4).

Christ, the high priest

The Book of Hebrews emphasizes another word-picture used by the church to explain Christ as Savior. Here Christ is called the high priest. "Since then we have a great high priest who has passed through the heavens, Jesus, the Son of God, let us hold fast our confession. For we have not a high priest who is unable to sympathize with our weaknesses, but one who in every respect has been tempted as we are, yet without sinning. Let us then with confidence draw near to the throne of grace, that we may receive mercy and find grace to help in time of need" (Hebrews 4:14-16).

In order to understand this reference to the high priest, you have to understand how the ancient Jews thought. They felt that every man owed God a holy life in return for God's gifts of love and protection. When a Jew had sinned, he tried to make amends for his unholiness. He did this by offering sacrifices—choosing birds and animals that had no physical flaws. Since a bird or animal could neither sin nor have faith, it was considered pure if it was physically perfect. The Jew believed that God, pleased by the sacrifice, would forgive the sinner. Usually the Jew took his sacrifices to the Temple, where the priest would slaughter them upon the altar and pray for the forgiveness of the sinner.

Once a year, the high priest went to a special place in the Temple where only he could go, a place called the "Holy of Holies." There, on this Day of Atonement, as it was called, the high priest offered sacrifices for all the people and sprinkled blood on the Ark of the Covenant, in which were kept the tablets of the Ten Commandments. Following this, he would go out to the people and sprinkle them with blood. They believed that the high priest's sacrifice to God on their behalf cleansed them from all their sin.

You can see why a Christian writer trying to interpret Christ to the Jews would talk to them in terms that were familiar to them. Christ, the writer of Hebrews is saying, is a better sacrifice to God than any animal or bird. He is a perfect human being, without sin, who offers himself for the sins of others. To carry the illustration a step further, he is the high priest himself, bringing his own perfect sacrifice to God on behalf of all people, whether they accept his ministry or not.

words that tell the story

No one of these word-pictures tells everything you want to know about Jesus Christ. Each picture, though, helps you develop a little more understanding of this great mystery of Christ's saving you. In addition to the word-pictures we have examined, many other words and phrases have become favorite expressions of Christians because they add to their understanding of what Jesus has done for us.

Among the words is *ransom*. Jesus said of himself, ". . . The Son of man came . . . to give his life as a ransom for many" (Matthew 20:28). Ransom is the act of releasing a captive by paying a price. Using this word tells you that Jesus gave himself as a payment to free you from the captivity of sin, death, and the Devil. The word *redeem* is related to this idea. To redeem is to recover. We are in debt to God; we owe him our love and complete loyalty. But we have allowed our love to shrink. We have given our loyalty to other things. We have become lost. Christ steps in, finds us and recovers us. He redeems us; he is our redeemer.

Another word is *reconcile*. The biblical word means "change." In Christ, the relationship between God and man is changed. Man's hostility toward God is changed to trust. Because Christ died for our sins, man and God are reconciled, restored to harmony.

Still another word is *expiation*. In addition to meaning atonement, this word also contains the idea of cleansing. By his sacrifice, Christ has not only atoned for our sins, but has washed them away, has cleansed us of them.

All these "pictures," these words and expressions, help you see something of what Christ has done for you. Jesus tells you that God does not condone or excuse sin; he hates sin. But God forgives because he loves the sinner. Your contentment, both in this life and in the life to come, depends upon your allowing Christ to bring you to God. You are really dependent upon him; no one else can help. He will be your friend, your Lord, your Savior, if you want him to serve you as he so freely offers.

If you believe these truths, then you can say with Luther, "I believe that Jesus Christ . . . has redeemed me, a lost and condemned person, saved me at great cost from sin, death, and the power of the devil—not with silver or gold, but with his holy and precious blood and his innocent suffering and death."

In the RCA Building in New York City, four murals portray the future of mankind. Three of the murals show man's conquests. The fourth depicts a lonely cross on a hill, with men hopefully looking up to it. Underneath are inscribed the words: "Man's ultimate destiny depends not upon whether he can learn new lessons and make new discoveries and conquests, but on his acceptance of the lesson taught him two thousand years ago." This is true. But Christ did more than teach a lesson; he made it possible for every human, born a child of God, to live as a child of God forever.

22

FROM CHRIST'S EASTER TO YOUR EASTER

Imagine that you were one of the disciples who saw Jesus die. What would it take to convince you that he was now alive again? Would you believe that he rose from the dead simply on the report of people you knew and trusted?

TO READ AND THINK ABOUT
Luke 24:13-35   On the Road to Emmaus
1 Corinthians 15:1-9   Resurrection Appearances
Acts 1:6-11   The Ascension
John 14:1-3   The Heavenly Home
Romans 8:31-39   More Than Conquerors
Luke 21:10-36   "Watch at All Times"
Matthew 25:31-46   The Judgment

---

doubting the resurrection

Thomas had a difficult time believing that Jesus ever came out of the tomb alive. He was not present when Jesus made his first appearance to the disciples in the Upper Room after his resurrection. He insisted he could not believe unless he could somehow touch the nail marks in Jesus' hands and feel the wound in his side.

Eight days later, when the disciples were again together in that Upper Room, Jesus appeared. Thomas' eyes were opened in amazement. No longer did he doubt; he knew that this was really the Master standing before him. He didn't reach out to touch the nail prints or the wounded side; he simply said, "My Lord and my God!" What Jesus said to Thomas, at this point, is especially interesting. He said, "Have you believed because you have seen me? Blessed are those who have not seen and yet believe" (John 20:28-29).

Jesus knew that many people would find it difficult to believe he had really risen from the dead. He understands how easy it is to doubt something you cannot see for yourself. However, Jesus doesn't want you to doubt that he lives. He wants to assure you that, in believing in his resurrection, you are blessed. To be blessed

means to be happy, joyous, highly favored. Those who accept Jesus as the risen Lord have an inner certainty and peace that only God can give.

Maybe you wish you could see Jesus face to face. But Jesus could not stay on earth and appear to all those who, like Thomas, have doubts. Some of his work would be undone if he remained. He told his disciples that he had to leave them so he could send the Holy Spirit to them. One day, he promised, he would come again. On the fortieth day after his resurrection Jesus went to a small hill with his faithful followers. There he talked to them about the coming of the Holy Spirit. He told them that they were to be his witnesses everywhere they went in the world. Then, suddenly, he was lifted from their sight. A cloud covered him and they saw him no more. While they stood there, not knowing what to do, two angels spoke to them: "Men of Galilee, why do you stand looking into heaven? This Jesus, who was taken up from you into heaven, will come in the same way as you saw him go into heaven" (Acts 1:10-11).

The disciples believed the angels. Their faith is reflected in the Apostles' Creed: "He ascended into heaven, And sitteth on the right hand of God the Father Almighty; From thence he shall come to judge the quick and the dead."

why did Jesus return to heaven?

The people of Jesus' day believed that the world was flat. According to this idea, heaven—where God was—had to be up beyond the clouds. Therefore, when the early Christians spoke of Jesus ascending, they thought of him as going up. Even though our understanding of the physical world is different from that of biblical times, the fact of the Ascension is still true. The important thing to remember is that Jesus returned to heaven, to the presence of God the Father. His earthly ministry was complete.

One of the reasons Jesus gave his disciples for his return to heaven was that he was going to prepare a place there for them. He promised that he would come again to earth so that all his followers would be with him, and that he would take them with him to heaven (see John 14:1-4).

Jesus also indicated that he returned to heaven so that he could continue to intercede for all his people. In a certain sense, he is a priest. Through him, we make our requests and desires known to God. As Jesus said, "I am the way, and the truth, and the life; no one comes to the Father, but by me" (John 14:6). In his last evening in the Upper Room, Jesus made this clear to the disciples. "Whatever you ask in my name, I will do it, that the Father may be glorified in the Son; if you ask anything in my name, I will do it" (John 14:13-14). Therefore, Jesus is your partner in prayer.

Jesus assured his followers that it was necessary for him to go away from them so that he could send the Holy Spirit into the world. He referred to the Holy Spirit as the Counselor. The Holy Spirit comes to guide and comfort you, to work faith in your heart, and to cause a new life to be born in you. The Holy Spirit also makes you conscious of your sin and your continual need of Jesus Christ as your Savior.

Christ returned to the Father so that he could be everywhere. As a man, Jesus could be in only one place at a time. When he was in Capernaum, therefore, he could not be in Jerusalem. Today Jesus Christ is in both Capernaum and Jerusalem. Today he is in Pittsburgh, Quebec, Berlin, and Moscow. Wherever his people are, Jesus comes to them. He is not with you in the physical form he had while he was the carpenter from Nazareth, but he is with you, nevertheless. He is with you through the Holy Spirit. Before he left the earth Jesus said, ". . . Lo, I am with you always, to the close of the age" (Matthew 28:20). Even now he keeps that promise.

belonging to Jesus

Some people have the impression that a Christian life is just a life of waiting. They think a Christian is simply marking time until he dies; then he will go to heaven and all the important things will start happening.

Luther doesn't agree. In explaining the Second Article of the Creed, he says about the work of Christ, "All this he has done that I may be his own, live under him in his kingdom, and serve him in everlasting righteousness, innocence, and blessedness, just as he is risen from the dead and lives and rules eternally. This is most certainly true." Luther is saying that you belong to Jesus now. You live under Jesus in his kingdom now. You serve Jesus in everlasting righteousness, innocence, and blessedness now.

Life eternal is a great gift which Christ gives to you. But don't think that it begins after you die. You started living the life eternal the day you became a Christian.

During his last week on earth, Jesus prayed a special prayer called the "High Priestly Prayer." In this prayer to the Father, Jesus speaks of life eternal. He tells you what it is. "And this is eternal life," he said, "that they (all his people) know thee the only true God, and Jesus Christ whom thou hast sent" (John 17:3).

Life eternal isn't just your independent life going on and on; it is life in partnership with Jesus Christ. Jesus wants to be your friend and constant companion. When you accept him and allow his godly influence to shape your personality, you have eternal life. You see, life eternal is measured not only by length but also by depth—the deep, solid foundation on which that life is built. Having Christ as your Lord gives your life permanence, importance, direction. Wherever you go, whatever you do, you know that your goal is to live to the glory of God and in loving service to your fellowmen. This is the kind of life Jesus lived; this is life eternal; this is living in the kingdom of God.

Wherever men believe in Jesus Christ and live with him, there the kingdom of God can be found. Though you still live in your community and go to your school and are proud to be a citizen of your country, you are simultaneously a citizen in the kingdom of God. Someday you will leave this earthly life and be with God in heaven because Jesus has given you the privilege of being in God's kingdom forever.

Luther said that Christians, as members of Christ's kingdom, serve Jesus "in everlasting righteousness, innocence, and blessedness." What does this mean? To serve Jesus in righteousness is to behave in the right way; to follow God's way of holiness. You want to choose good over evil, faith over disobedience to God's will. To serve him in innocence is to be a forgiven person, as though you had never sinned at all. Your sin is forgotten when God forgives you. You are once more pure and innocent. To serve him in blessedness is to serve with a happy and willing heart. You do it because you want to. You do it in love and thankfulness. You are happy that you can serve Jesus Christ.

when Jesus comes again

Someday Jesus Christ is coming again to judge the living and the dead. No one knows the day or the hour when he will come. But Jesus told us we should live in constant readiness, for when he comes every man will face him and be judged in terms of whether or not he is living as a forgiven son of God. You are responsible for your life. Your parents cannot make excuses for you. No one can. Your whole life will be an open book before Jesus Christ. In some ways, this is comparable to a general's unexpected inspection tour of a military base. As he walks through the barracks and reviews the troops on the parade ground, he can tell immediately which men have kept themselves and their equipment in top condition. And he knows that these are the good soldiers, on whom he can depend.

Does Jesus' coming as a judge frighten you? It need not—not if you belong to him, if you are living your life in his kingdom and are serving him. Instead of fright and fear, you will feel joy and gladness because a friend has come. No one is afraid of his friends.

In Paul's day, many people wanted to know what kind of body they would have in the resurrection. You probably have wondered the same thing. Read what Paul answered in 1 Corinthians 15:35-44. He says that your resurrection body is a spiritual body. It is different from your present physical body in that it will be imperishable; it will have a new glory and power. But you will still be you. It will be like the resurrection body of Jesus—not limited as much as the physical body was, but still recognizable. Jesus' disciples knew him when he appeared to them. Even Thomas knew the Master when he finally saw him face to face.

The body you now have is subject to accidents and can be destroyed. When Jesus comes you will be given a new body, a resurrection body which nothing can harm or destroy.

heaven

When you think of heaven, think of a place where you will be with Jesus and with all those who have followed him. Don't worry because you can't locate it geographically or describe it in detail. Jesus purposely told us little about heaven. He did not want our desire for the perfection of heaven to be so strong that we would give up the joy and satisfactions that are possible in this imperfect life we now lead.

Many have tried to paint word-pictures of heaven. During the terrible Roman persecutions of the early Christian church, a man called John wrote a message of courage to all those who were suffering torture and death. This message, which is the last book of the New Testament, is called Revelation. Writing near the end of the first century from the island of Patmos, John encouraged his readers to remain faithful to Christ no matter what the consequences. He painted heaven in glowing terms to make the faithful realize that although they might lose their earthly lives for their faith, an even richer life awaited them in the presence of God. In Revelation 21, John describes heaven—which he calls "the new Jerusalem"—as a city with walls of precious mineral like jasper. Each of the twelve gates of the city is manned by angels and is made of a single pearl. John says this city of pure gold is built on twelve foundations adorned with beautiful and rare jewels, and that on these foundations appear the names of the twelve apostles. Old spirituals reflect these ideas with their reference to "pearly gates" and "golden streets."

Actually, the only accurate description we can make of heaven is that there is great beauty there. There is no more ugliness or pain or suffering or wrong because you are with God. What more do we need to know?

you are important

The fact that Jesus is coming again is another indication of how important you are to him. Jesus is not content with what he has already done for you, in making possible forgiveness and preparing the way for you to enjoy life eternal. He will come again to escort you personally into the presence of the Father.

Everything about you is important in the eyes of God. God is interested in your every deed and every thought, in every minute of your life. His vigil over you is continuous. Nothing about you or about what you do goes unnoticed. God's love is constant. It makes a lot of difference to him what you do and why you do it. He is counting on you to be his forever.

23

"I BELIEVE"

You've probably never heard of Shimabuku on the island of Okinawa in the South Pacific. It's an obscure little town. Only a few hundred people live there.

Yet some American Marines, who landed in Okinawa in 1945, will never forget Shimabuku. Advance patrols pushing inland met two little old men who stood bowing before them and asking to speak. The battle-hardened veterans looked at each other in amazement. Then they motioned to the old men to go ahead and speak. This is the story they heard.

```
TO READ AND THINK ABOUT
              (Note power in faith)
Matthew 8:5-13    For the Centurion
Matthew 9:18-26   For the Ruler
Matthew 9:27-31   For Two Blind Men
Matthew 15:21-28  For the Woman of Tyre
Luke 23:39-43     For the Repentant Criminal
Hebrews 11:1-16   From Adam to Abraham
Hebrews 12:1-2    The Cloud of Witnesses
```

what Jesus did in shimabuku

In 1915 an American missionary stopped at Shimabuku enroute to Japan. He did not stay long, but his visit made an impression on two brothers, Shosei Kima and Mojon. After listening to the missionary speak glowingly about Christ, they became Christians. Before he left, the missionary gave the brothers a Bible.

In the intervening years, Shosei Kima and Mojon carefully read and reread the New Testament. They came to know and love Jesus Christ more and more. They even tried to apply the teachings of Jesus Christ to their whole community.

In time, Shosei Kima and Mojon shared their faith with the other people in the village. Every man, woman, and child in Shimabuku eventually became a Christian. By the time the Marines came, Shosei Kima was the head man of the village and Mojon its chief teacher. They were out on the dusty road to welcome the Americans as fellow Christians.

The advance patrol sent for the chaplain. Together with other officers, he toured the city. They found homes and streets spotlessly clean, the people gentle and intelligent, healthy and happy. These people had a Christian relationship with God which made a difference in the way they lived. Shimabuku was far different from many other Okinawan villages, which were unbelievably poor and filthy.

Naturally, the Americans were astonished at what they saw, too astonished to speak. Shosei Kima and Mojon misunderstood; they thought the Americans were disappointed. Humbly the brothers bowed, "We are sorry if we seem a backward people. We have tried our best, honored sirs, to follow the Bible and live like Jesus. Perhaps if you will show us how . . ."

Later, one of the army sergeants said to a war correspondent, "I can't figure it—this kind of people coming out of only a Bible and a couple of old guys who wanted to live like Jesus! Maybe we've been using the wrong kind of weapon to make the world over."

what Jesus did for the centurion

Do you remember the Roman centurion whose faith impressed Jesus? This soldier came to Jesus one day seeking help for a servant who was paralyzed. Jesus agreed to go with him and heal his servant. The centurion, however, protested that he was unworthy of having Jesus come into his home. If Christ would only say the word, he knew his servant would be healed. As an officer in the Roman army, he gave orders which he expected to be obeyed. He knew Jesus had great power. If Jesus would just speak a word of healing, he felt sure the servant would become well again. Jesus responded warmly, "Truly, I say to you, not even in Israel have I found such faith." Because of the centurion's faith, the servant was healed at the very hour Jesus spoke (Matthew 8:5-13).

what is faith?

You could cite many examples of people whose lives were changed by the influence of Christ. You could tell about many marvelous things that happened to people who were Christians. But don't fall into the trap of thinking that your faith is a way of getting God to do things for you or a way of guaranteeing a life without problems. Faith is not an insurance policy against tragedy and heartbreak. Faith gives you the strength and courage to bear these experiences when they come. Faith is not a practical tool that you use because you know it helps bring sanitation to a village like

Shimabuku, or healing for an afflicted servant; faith is a whole way of life with Jesus as your unseen, but ever-present, partner. Don't confuse the by-products of faith with faith itself. Faith is nothing more or less than saying "Yes" to God's offer of help to you through Jesus Christ: "Yes, I will accept him as my friend and Lord"— "Yes, I will follow where he leads the way."

Let's make another point. Faith is more than saying you accept something as being true. You could say, "I believe the earth is round instead of flat," or "I believe jets can fly faster than the speed of sound." You accept these facts on the evidence others have given you even though you have never measured the earth or flown a jet.

Some people think they have faith in God because they accept the fact that there is a God. Or they think they have faith in Christ because they do not deny that Christ once lived among men, was crucified, and rose again from the dead. Simply to say that there is a God and that Christ once lived on earth doesn't really mean your life is attached to his. You could easily believe that there is such a thing as an electric light and still go on burning a kerosene lamp in your home.

When you confess your faith in the Creed, you say, "I believe in God the Father . . . I believe in Jesus Christ . . . I believe in the Holy Spirit." "Believing in" means trust, dependence, loyalty, obedience—this is faith. Not only do you accept the truth about God, but you go a step further and give yourself to him even as he has given himself to you.

In the marriage service, a man and a woman vow their loyalty and undying love to each other. With these vows they literally give themselves to each other. They are married. The bride and bridegroom are no longer two people; they are "one flesh."

The vows of the marriage service illustrate something significant about the nature of faith. In love, Christ gives himself to you. In faith, you accept him as your Lord. When you use Luther's words "I believe that Jesus Christ . . . is my Lord," you are indeed giving yourself to Christ as a loyal follower of his way. Faith is a total commitment of your life to Christ. In faith, you trust him, you depend upon him, you live with him. In faith, your will is surrendered to his will and your desires reflect his desires.

To use an old acrostic, you could simply express faith this way:

F*orsaking*
A*ll*
I
T*rust*
H*im*

Have you ever wondered what Jesus meant when he said, "For whoever would save his life will lose it, and whoever loses his life for my sake will find it" (Matthew 16:25), and "Whoever would be first among you must be slave of all" (Mark 10:44)?

The way to find life is to lose life. The way to get ahead in the world is to take the back seat. These statements seem to contradict popular opinion. You might say, "What kind of nonsense is this?"

But Jesus was not speaking nonsense; he was showing us the real nature of faith. Faith is losing yourself in Jesus Christ, surrendering your life to him. In Christ, you really find yourself; you discover your real potentialities. You catch a glimpse of how you can use your life to God's glory and in service to your fellowmen. Faith breeds a certain humbleness. When you have faith, you share God's loving concern for every human being regardless of his nationality, his economic level, or the color of his skin. This concern will lead you to seek ways in which you can help others. Jesus also said, "Let your light so shine before men, that they may see your good works and give glory to your Father who is in heaven" (Matthew 5:16).

risks

There is something risky about faith. Let's face it. You are risking everything upon one whom you have not seen.

To take risks in life is not unusual. You take many risks every day. Sitting down on a chair can be risky; it might collapse under you. When you eat a candy bar you take a risk; it might give you a toothache. When you read a book, you risk getting wrong ideas. Even telling a secret to a friend may be risky; he may not keep your secret. Yet only by taking these risks can you have rest and food, mental stimulation, close friends.

When you take the risk of faith, you put your trust in the gifts of God—and God will make that faith count. The people of Shimabuku took a risk, and discovered a new life in their village. The centurion found his servant healed because he was willing to risk putting his confidence in the power of Christ. When you give your faith to Christ you do so knowing that he is completely trustworthy. He will never let you down. He is your Lord.

Part Seven

Luther's Discovery of Christ

24

THE LAW STUDENT WHO BECAME A MONK

Have you ever gone mountain climbing?

It's a great thrill to stand on a mountaintop and look out over the surrounding countryside. But it takes a lot of strength and effort to reach the top. On the way up you get tired and you wonder if the view will be worth the strain. Then you catch a glimpse of the peak. With renewed zeal, you resume climbing. Reaching the top demands all the stamina you have. So you keep telling yourself that you can make it; you force your muscles to keep working. Then, at last, the top—the joy of conquest and accomplishment!

> ## TO READ AND THINK ABOUT
> Psalm 6   David Weary in Sin
> Psalm 38   David Asking for God's Help
> Psalm 51   David Confessing His Sins
> Psalm 32   David Glad in Forgiveness
> Romans 1:18-25   Under the Wrath of God
> Jeremiah 13:23   The Evil Cannot Do Good
> Romans 5:3-5   From Suffering to Hope

Some people think of God as dwelling on some great height. They feel they can reach God if they try hard enough, if they discipline themselves, if they force their minds and bodies to obey all of his laws. They know that the summit where God lives is far away and hard to reach. The spiritual pilgrimage, therefore, will demand their best efforts.

To these persons, God is up and man is below. They believe that man can know and be with God only by working his way up to where God is.

Did you know that, for many years, Martin Luther thought this was the way to be a Christian, to work his way up to God? For a long time, he tried hard to climb to God's presence by being good and doing those things he thought would please God. Then he found out, to his dismay, that neither he nor any other man could ever succeed in working his way up to God. But as a result of this painful discovery, he came to know who Christ really was and what faith in Christ meant to the Christian. He felt compelled to share his new understandings with the indifferent church of his day—and in so doing, he changed the course of history.

Since God chose Martin Luther to remind Christians of some great biblical truths which had been almost forgotten, it is good to know something about this man for whom our church is proudly named. We are indebted to Luther in so many ways. We sing the hymns that he wrote and study the Catechism that he prepared. Most of all, we are fortunate in having him to lead us to a deeper understanding of the importance of our faith in Christ.

luther's early years

The son of hardworking peasants, Luther was born November 10, 1483, in Eisleben, Germany. When he was a small boy, the Luthers moved to Mansfeld where young Martin went to school. His father Hans, now working in the mines, had high hopes for his son.

Hans Luther's dream was that Martin would someday become a prosperous lawyer. He encouraged his son to enter the University of Erfurt. Four years later, Martin graduated and immediately began his law studies. The future looked secure, and Hans Luther's dream seemed about to come true.

Not long after he started studying law, Luther gave a supper for some of his friends. It was a happy, festive affair. However, as the guests were about to leave, Luther announced that he was leaving the university; he was dropping his law studies. To his friends' amazement, he went on to explain that he was going to enter an Augustinian monastery in Erfurt the next day and work toward becoming a monk. His friends thought he had taken leave of his senses; they could not understand his decision.

luther becomes a monk

Why did Luther want to spend his life behind cloistering walls? He had been a happy, jolly student at the university, well liked by everyone. The life of the monastery would be quiet, lonely, and strict. Luther had a warm, outgoing personality; he enjoyed knowing and being with people. The monastic life was a withdrawal from the world, a breaking of almost all social ties. He would live in a somber cloister, having contact only with a few fellow monks. Luther was not unmindful of his parents' hopes and dreams for him. He must have known that he would be hurting his father particularly. But he had made his decision; he had some very good reasons for doing so.

In Luther's day the people were taught to believe that Christ

was not only a gracious redeemer; he was also an angry judge. Escaping the anger of Christ became a great concern of people. Many believed that the persons most able to escape the fierce anger of Christ were monks, who were spending their time in prayer, confession, and good works. Christ couldn't possibly be unforgiving toward men who lived perfect lives like that!

Luther had once seen, over a church altar, a painting which depicted contented monks and priests aboard a ship on its way to heaven. In the waves, laymen of the church were struggling desperately to hold onto the ship as it moved through the waters of life. Many were unable to maintain their grasp and so were drowning in the sea. It was a frightening picture of what could happen to a person who was not a professional worker in the church.

On another occasion, Luther had seen Prince William of Anhalt wandering through the village streets like a common beggar. Luther remembered how this royal prince, who was trying to be a holy man, looked. "With my own eyes I saw him . . . He had so worn himself down by fasting and vigil that he looked like a death's-head, mere bone and skin. No one could look upon him without feeling ashamed of his own life." Luther was haunted by the feeling that he would never be worthy of God's blessing, that God could never accept and love him the way he was.

In the early summer of the year he entered law school, Luther spent a week with his parents in Mansfeld. On his way back to Erfurt, he rode into a severe thunderstorm. Thunder rumbled; lightning zigzagged violently across the sky. One bolt crashed close to the horse he was riding and Luther was thrown to the ground. Terrified, he felt that the wrath of God was striking him down. Since his father was a miner, he cried out in terror to St. Anne, the patron saint of the miners, "St. Anne, help me! I will become a monk." When the storm subsided, he was conscious of his promise, which lay like a heavy weight on his shoulders.

These experiences shaped Luther's decision to enter a monastery. He thought he was obeying God. Underlying his decision were many doubts and fears. He didn't know how God felt about him; he feared his life was not pleasing to God. He doubted that he could ever please God unless he did many good works. He thought that by joining a monastery, he would be more likely to get close to God and so escape the terrible punishment of hell.

in the monastery

As a monk, Luther resolved to try all the good works the church had established. He fasted, sometimes going for three days without food. A monk was supposed to spend part of each day in prayer, but Luther daily prayed much longer than was required. Sometimes

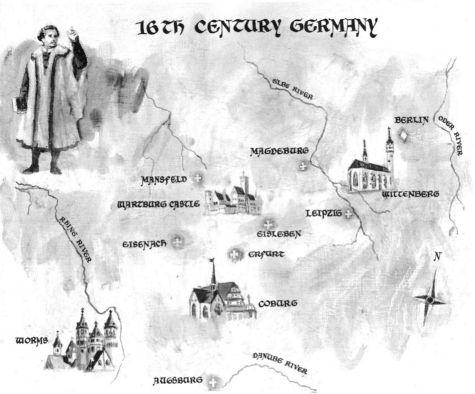

ELBE RIVER

BERLIN

ODER RIVER

MAGDEBURG

WITTENBERG

MANSFELD

WARTBURG CASTLE

LEIPZIG

EISENACH

EISLEBEN

ERFURT

N

RHINE RIVER

COBURG

WORMS

DANUBE RIVER

AUGSBURG

at night he would throw aside his blankets in the freezing cold to punish himself for his sins. He thought he must please God with his self-control, that he must make God feel merciful toward him.

In later years, Luther commented wryly on his days in the monastery. "I was a good monk, and I kept the rule of my order so strictly that I may say that if ever a monk got to heaven by his monkery it was I. All my brothers in the monastery who knew me will bear me out. If I had kept on any longer, I should have killed myself with vigils, prayers, reading, and other work."

After a year of this life, Luther was directed by his superiors to study for the priesthood. He was only twenty-four years old when he was ordained a priest of the church. A few weeks later he celebrated his first Mass. It was during this joyous occasion that he had a strange experience. As the service progressed, he became more and more terror-stricken. How dare he, a sinner, stand in the presence of the holy God? How could such a sinful man ever stand before the altar and address Almighty God?

Slowly Luther was moving toward the first of two great discoveries in his life. He was finding out that he could not satisfy God. No matter what he did, he was always conscious of his sinfulness. At times he would say to himself, "I have done nothing wrong today." Immediately, questions would arise in his mind. "Have you

153

fasted enough?" "Are you poor enough?" The peace of mind he expected did not come. God was too holy, too far above him; he did not have the capacity to do what God required. Every attempt to reach God, to please God, was ending in dismal failure. Discouraged, he came to the conclusion that flesh and blood can never rise above itself.

a roman holiday

When he was twenty-seven, Luther went to Rome on business for the monastery. He was delighted to make the six-month journey. Going to Rome was making a pilgrimage to the "Eternal City"; this was certainly a good work. Filled with zeal to find and please God, he roamed excitedly about the city trying to see all the church's treasures. There were many famous, supposedly authentic, relics—among them a piece of Moses' burning bush, the chains of Paul, one of the thirty coins paid to Judas Iscariot, eleven thorns from Christ's crown, a hair from the head of the Virgin Mary.

Of course, he would climb the famous Pilate staircase, the very staircase of Pilate's palace which Jesus had climbed on Good Friday. There were great heavenly rewards for this kind of holy exercise.

Luther believed, as did the church of his day, that when an individual died he went to purgatory, a sort of way station on the road to heaven. (Our church believes, instead, that when Christians die they go directly to be with God.) In purgatory, the individual suffered for his sins until he had atoned for them and could go to heaven. However, his friends and family could, by doing good works, earn "merits" which would shorten his stay in purgatory.

There is a story that Luther, hoping to do something that would please God and, at the same time, help his grandfather in purgatory, went to Pilate's staircase. He climbed it on his hands and knees, stopping at each step to kiss it and to offer a prayer. But by the time he reached the top, he was filled with doubts. "Who knows whether it is so," he wondered, "that a man can earn merits like this?" Troubled, he rose to his feet and walked back down.

Rome, to which Luther had gone with such hopes and aspirations, was a great disappointment in other ways, too. Not only was he bothered with serious doubts, but he was shocked to see the worldly conduct of some of the priests. Their behavior, far from holy, made him question their sincerity. He returned home thoroughly discouraged. Even a pilgrimage to Rome had failed to bring him any closer to God. What could he do to save himself?

Many people have found themselves in the same predicament when they realize their sinfulness and feel that nothing they can do will make it up to God. Perhaps sometimes you feel this way, too.

154

25

"HERE I STAND"

Luther's feelings of sinfulness and unworthiness continued to haunt him upon his return from Rome. He needed some big task to take his mind off himself, and he found one the next year. Frederick the Wise, who ruled Saxony (a duchy in Northwest Germany), was looking for a professor at his new university in Wittenberg. Martin Luther was given the assignment.

TO READ AND THINK ABOUT

Luke 15:11-32   The Boy Who Returned
Romans 1:16-17   The Gospel
Romans 3:21-26   Justification by Faith
Romans 6:19-23   The Free Gift of God
1 Corinthians 1:18-31   The Cross Is Power
Galatians 3:15-21   Salvation Is Not by the Law
Galatians 6:14-15   Glorying in the Cross

---

to wittenberg

At the university, Luther lectured on the Bible. He was a forceful teacher and became quite popular with his students. He spent much time in Bible study, and came to love the book and its messages. But he had many difficulties in reconciling what the Bible had to say with what the church taught.

Johann von Staupitz, the head of the Augustinian order of monks, knew Luther was having problems. Generously he advised Luther to study for his doctor's degree in the teachings of the church. Staupitz was a good friend, gladly giving of his own time to help Luther find solutions to his doubts. He suggested that, above all else, the young professor learn to love God; he had to if he were to find peace. But Luther simply could not love God. How could he love a God who was angry with him, who would judge him and condemn him to hell? Luther commented, "I was . . . driven to the very abyss of despair so that I wished I had never been created. Love God? I hated him!"

what is God's righteousness?

It was not until the spring of 1513 that things began to change. Luther was preparing a series of lectures on the Book of Psalms.

He came to the word "righteousness" in many of the psalms. Righteousness meant being free from all sin, worry, and guilt. The righteous man was holy before God, worthy of God. Every time he came upon this word, he was disturbed by his own doubts and fears. He could not think of himself as being righteous. Yet he believed God wanted him and all men to be righteous.

To understand the word "righteousness" better, he decided to study Paul's Letter to the Romans. With amazement, he paused at the words, "For I am not ashamed of the gospel: it is the power of God for salvation to every one who has faith, to the Jew first and also to the Greek. For in it the righteousness of God is revealed through faith for faith; as it is written, 'He who through faith is righteous shall live' " (Romans 1:16-17).

Suddenly Luther understood the truth. When the Bible is describing the "power of God," it isn't speaking of a power God bottles up in himself. It is describing a power God gives to people. Likewise, when the Bible is describing righteousness, it isn't speaking of a righteousness which belongs to God alone, but rather the righteousness God gives to man. This righteousness is the free gift of God. No one can earn it. When God forgives a person, he makes that person righteous as though he had never sinned at all.

God in Christ comes to man

Luther had already realized that it was impossible to please God by his own efforts.

Now he discovered that he had been wrong in assuming that he or anyone else could climb up to where God was; instead, God comes down to men. In Jesus Christ, God came to men dramatically, giving not only forgiveness for his sins but righteousness as well to each person who accepts these gifts.

How can man have peace with God? How is man redeemed and saved from the curse of selfishness, from the punishment he deserves for his sins? Now Luther had the answer to these problems. It was so simple—God's *love*. God was not a tyrant you could bribe with a sackful of good works. Instead, God was like the father in Jesus' Parable of the Prodigal Son (Luke 15:11-32). Remember how Jesus described the father running out to greet and forgive his wayward son? The boy had gone away, selfishly seeking to live the way he wanted. But he soon realized that he had been wrong. Sadly returning home, realizing that he didn't deserve it but hoping for some small favor, the son was overwhelmed to have his father hug him and forgive him and treat him as though he had never been away. In Christ, God was coming to embrace all people who were sorry for their sins.

Through his study of the Bible, Luther realized that God was calling him to faith in Jesus Christ. For Jesus Christ had done everything necessary to bring God and men together. Nothing more need be done except for Luther to put his complete trust in Jesus Christ as his Lord.

justification by faith

Luther's great discovery that God in Christ comes to men freely, forgiving them and accepting them as his sons, is called "justification by faith." The meaning of "justify," in this sense, is to "release from the guilt of sin and make righteous." "Justification by faith" means that it is our faith in God, and not our good works, that makes us righteous and frees us from sin. The church in Luther's day had forgotten that the most important thing for man was to love and trust God. It had emphasized doing the right things so hard that it had lost sight of the reason for doing them.

kinship with paul

Luther came to feel very close to the apostle Paul. It was Paul's Letter to the Romans that had opened his eyes to the truth about God's love. And the more he read Paul's letters, the more Luther realized that Paul had had a similar experience to his own. At one time, Paul had possessed all the qualifications which were thought to give a man special standing before God. He was born a Hebrew of the tribe of Benjamin. He was one of the Pharisees, a group extremely zealous to do all the works of the Jewish Law. He had been very strict in obeying whatever the Law of God commanded. He had even helped to persecute the early Christians. Yet, says Paul, "Whatever gain I had, I counted as loss for the sake of Christ. Indeed I count everything as loss because of the surpassing worth of knowing Jesus Christ my Lord" (Philippians 3:7-8).

Coming to know Jesus Christ as God's fullest expression of love and concern for men was the turning point in Luther's life as it had been in Paul's. Life now had new dimensions, opportunities, and challenges. Life was rich and satisfying now that the heavy burden of guilt and despair had been lifted from him.

The four years following Luther's momentous discovery were quietly busy. He spent much of his time in Bible study; he was busy thinking, writing, and lecturing. He must have been working day and night, for he wrote a friend, "I could use two secretaries."

In a sense, this quiet was deceptive. Luther was just beginning to study the church and its teachings carefully in the light of his newly uncovered Bible truths. An explosion was coming soon.

indulgences

In the fall of 1517, a man named John Tetzel, a seller of indulgences, appeared near Wittenberg. An indulgence was a slip of paper bearing the signature of the pope. By buying this little piece of paper a person could receive assurance that his sins of the future would be forgiven, or that some member of his family or a friend would have less time to spend in purgatory. Remember, in those days practically everybody believed that purgatory was a real place where people went when they died and that, by doing special good works for God, you could shorten someone's stay there. Buying an indulgence was considered a very good work, although the amount of time its purchase actually cut from someone's stay in purgatory depended upon how much money you paid.

At this time, Pope Leo needed money badly for the building of St. Peter's Cathedral in Rome, and indulgences were a good way of getting funds. He promoted the sale of indulgences all over Germany. John Tetzel was one of his star salesmen. Coming into a community, Tetzel would gather a crowd and describe for them the terrors of eternal flames in which persons now dead were suffering. Then he would add:

As soon as the coin in the coffer rings,
The soul from purgatory springs.

He sold indulgences at a fantastic rate.

When Luther saw people coming back to Wittenberg feeling they had helped their loved ones in purgatory, he was distressed. This was not faith in Christ; it was faith in a piece of paper! He had to do something to bring men to their senses. All Saints' Day, November 1, was close at hand. This day was observed in the church as a time to recall great Christians who had lived in the past. It made people mindful of members of their own family who were now dead. On October 31, 1517, the evening before All Saints' Day, Luther strode to the door of the Castle Church where public notices were displayed. On that door, he nailed a list of ninety-five theses (or arguments) protesting the sale of indulgences and questioning other unscriptural practices of the church. The Ninety-Five Theses were intended for scholars who often spent All Saints' Day debating current problems or matters of theology. Luther planned to give the scholars at Wittenberg something to think about.

Luther didn't realize how many people soon would be thinking, arguing, and discussing the questions he had raised. Someone printed copies of the Ninety-Five Theses and distributed them all over Germany. Like a prairie fire, Luther's ideas spread across the country and were eagerly taken up by men from all walks of life. Luther was surprised and pleased at this reaction.

How did the pope and officials of the church feel about all this?

At first, they ignored Luther and his point of view. They were busy with other things. However, when many pamphlets, sermons, and tracts began to appear, all bearing the name of Martin Luther, Pope Leo paid more attention. He ordered Cardinal Cajetan to get Luther to stop these writings questioning the practices of the church.

In October, 1518, Luther was ordered by the cardinal to appear in Augsburg. Obediently, Luther went to meet Cajetan. The cardinal urged him to take back what he had written. Boldly Luther refused. Lunching later with Staupitz, who had come with Luther to Augsburg, the cardinal said, "I am not going to talk with him any more. His eyes are as deep as a lake, and there are amazing speculations in his head."

The cardinal urged Staupitz, as head of the Augustinian monastery, to make Luther renounce his writings. Staupitz tried and failed. Not knowing what else to do, he released Luther from his vows as a monk. Now the professor was on his own.

excommunication

Luther continued writing. In 1520, of the 208 books published in all Germany, 133 of them were written by Luther. It was in this year, too, that the pope decided to excommunicate Luther. Excommunication means to be denied the privilege of participating in the Sacrament of Holy Communion. In effect, it means being thrown out of the church. Luther was labeled a heretic, a man who distorted Christian doctrines. Further, people were expected to avoid him; a heretic was supposed to have no friends. The pope charged Luther with forty-one heresies. The charge said, in part, "We can no longer suffer the serpent to creep through the field of the Lord. The books of Martin Luther which contain these errors are to be examined and burned."

The name used for the official papers which declared Luther's punishment was the "Bull of Excommunication." (A Bull is a formal decree, usually issued by the pope.) This document reached Luther in October, 1520. He was given sixty days to retract his damaging statements. What would he do?

The answer came on the night of December 10. At Wittenberg, a group of university students gathered around a roaring bonfire. Into the fire, people threw books written by Luther's enemies. Suddenly Luther appeared at the fire and calmly tossed a little book into the flames. It was the Bull of Excommunication. He was not going to change his mind or his ideas.

What to do with Luther became one of the problems which faced Charles V, the young emperor of the Holy Roman Empire, when he came into Germany late in 1520. Charles hesitated in making any decision. He needed the help of all the Germans in his war with France, and he knew that Luther was very popular. To punish Luther openly might mean the loss of troops and support for his military campaigns. On the other hand, he couldn't very well ignore the growing support for a man who had been excommunicated and labeled a heretic.

diet of worms

Finally, in 1521, Charles called for a diet to meet in the city of Worms. A diet was a gathering of the princes of the different states and cities. Their task was to pass judgment on the various problems confronting the Empire. Luther was summoned to appear before this group. Many of his friends urged him not to answer the summons. They remembered that a century earlier John Huss, who also had sought to reform the church, had trustingly appeared before the council at Constance; he was martyred. Luther's enemies called Luther "the Saxon Huss." His friends feared that he, like Huss, might be burned at the stake. But Luther went to Worms anyway, secure in his belief that God would take care of him.

When Luther appeared before the Imperial Diet, he expected to have an opportunity to tell what he believed and why. The emperor sat on a throne at one end of the room, with his officers and the representatives of the pope about him. In the center of the room was a table on which were copies of the books Luther had written. Luther was ready to explain his views. Instead the spokesman for the emperor asked him two questions. First, would Luther admit he was the author of the books on the table? Second, would he renounce them? To the first question Luther, without hesitation, answered, "Yes." The second question was not so easy to handle. Luther asked for more time to prepare his answer, and was given until the next day. Luther spent the night in prayer.

The next day, the hall was crowded. When his time came to speak, Luther began an explanation of the types of writings which were on the table. He was rudely interrupted, "Do you or do you not repudiate your books and the errors which they contain?"

Then slowly came Luther's reply. "Since then Your Majesty and your lordships desire a simple reply, I will answer without horns and without teeth. Unless I am convicted by Scripture and plain reason—I do not accept the authority of popes and councils, for they have contradicted each other—my conscience is captive to the Word of God. I cannot and I will not recant anything, for to go against conscience is neither right nor safe. God help me. Amen."

The diet was in confusion. Charles stalked out in anger. Back in his room Luther paced the floor in sadness, saying over and over again, "I am through! I am through!"

26

THE REFORMER AT WORK

Luther had burned the pope's order of excommunication. He had stood courageously before the emperor and refused to renounce his writings. Now what? Would he be put to death like a common criminal? People in high authority don't like to be told they are wrong.

TO READ AND THINK ABOUT
(*Note the importance of God's Word*)
Psalm 19:7-14   More Desirable Than Gold
Psalm 119:9-16   Keeping the Way Pure
Psalm 119:105-112   A Lamp and a Light
Isaiah 55:6-11   It Is Not Empty
2 Timothy 3:14-17   Scripture Inspired by God
Hebrews 4:12-13   Sharper Than a Sword
1 Peter 1:22-25   God's Word Abides Forever

under the ban of the emperor

After Luther left the city of Worms to return to his Wittenberg home, the emperor issued a proclamation. In this imperial edict, Charles forbade anyone to have any dealings with Luther the outlaw. He called on all his loyal subjects to seize Luther and bring him to the proper authorities. He made buying, selling, printing, reading, or possessing Luther's writings a crime. Anyone guilty of disobeying these laws could be punished by death.

Luther was saved from harm through the unexpected intervention of the ruler of Saxony, Frederick the Elector. Luther lived in Wittenberg, which was in Saxon territory and Frederick would not permit one of his subjects to be treated cruelly by the emperor or anyone else. Further, not fully trusting the emperor, he feared that something "unfortunate" might happen to Luther.

Quickly and quietly Frederick developed a plan. As Luther and his friends were riding back to Wittenberg, a band of the Elector's soldiers hid in a forest along the way. When Luther came by, they attacked his party. Dragging him roughly from the wagon in which he was riding and mounting him on a horse, they carried him away. Deep into the Thuringian mountains, the soldiers rode in silence. Luther thought he was going to be killed. Finally, just before midnight, they rode up a high, wooded hill to Wartburg Castle. The castle was to be Luther's haven, a good hiding place until the opposition to this young professor and his challenging ideas died down.

During his confinement in Wartburg Castle Luther dressed like a knight, grew a beard, and was called "Junker George." He kept himself busy by studying and writing. One of his greatest projects was translating the New Testament into German.

luther and the bible

Luther was a man of the Bible. Actually, it was his belief that the Bible was the source of all the church's authority that had brought him into conflict with the church. He sincerely believed that whenever the teachings and practices of the church conflicted with the Bible the church was wrong.

Luther disagreed vehemently with the idea that only the church could interpret the Bible properly. He was convinced that every man should have the privilege of reading it for himself. This meant that the Bible had to be available to everyone in his own language. With speed and great zeal he worked; and within three months, he had translated the New Testament into German. (The Old Testament would take longer; he needed help with the Hebrew language from scholarly friends. The translation of the whole Bible was not completed until 1534.)

To Luther, the Bible was central to Christian faith and life. He immersed himself in the Bible, absorbing its teachings. The people of the Bible were his friends, people with whom he was acquainted. He knew God as they did. In the pages of the Bible, he had made the greatest discovery of his life: the discovery that God reached down to him in Jesus Christ.

There was little time to rest in the secluded castle. He was constantly confronted with problems. Many people, admiring his courageous support of truth, looked to him for leadership. Reports were coming in describing the rapid changes taking place in Wittenberg. A fellow professor named Carlstadt was guiding the people in developing new practices. Some changes were good: German was being used in church services instead of Latin; priests, monks, and nuns were now allowed to marry and live normal lives. Other changes were not so good: Mobs were breaking into churches overturning altars, smashing pictures, and destroying images; pictures, statues, images, even music and organs in churches were being condemned; vestments for the clergy were being discarded.

luther returns to wittenberg

Finally, Luther could no longer stand his isolation. He returned to Wittenberg on March 6, 1522, and immediately went to work. In his sermons, he emphasized that the most important task of the church was proclaiming the Word of God. God's Word would change the hearts of men. Other concerns of the church, such as orders of worship, language, monastic vows, were matters of personal choice. To Luther, these were the nonessentials.

Through his preaching and pastoral ministry, Luther showed that he was not a radical who wanted to discard all the traditions of the church just for the sake of beginning anew. He suggested that all customs and practices should be analyzed carefully in the light of faith in Jesus Christ and the authority of the Bible. If any practices in the church conflicted with this faith then, of course, the practices must be changed. However, if there were no conflict, then those customs and practices which had values in the Christian life should be retained.

the service

Luther's point of view can be illustrated by looking at the changes that were made in the chief service of worship, "the Mass." The word "Mass" means "body." When the priest lifted the bread and the wine at the altar during the Sacrament of Holy Communion, the Roman Catholic church believed he was repeating Christ's sacrifice of his body and blood on the cross. Further, they believed that the bread and the wine actually became Christ's body and blood in the service. Consequently, because of the danger of spilling Christ's precious blood, the wine was not given to laymen. They received only bread when they communed. Generally, the layman was a spectator at the worship service. The liturgy was all in Latin. The priest and the choir, if there was one, did all the singing. But going to Mass was believed to be a good work which would help save a man, so the average person went regularly.

Luther and his friends began to make changes in the Mass so that it would reflect more accurately the teachings of the New Testament. Since we believe that Christ sacrificed his life willingly on Calvary, making one sacrifice for all of mankind, then no man— not even a priest—can ever sacrifice Christ again. Therefore, this part of the service was dropped—and the wine, as well as the bread, was given to every worshiper. Luther carefully pointed out, that although the person who eats the bread and drinks the wine receives the real presence of Jesus Christ in his heart, the bread and wine remain bread and wine. The changing of the elements is a symbolic one; there is no magic involved. And because Luther believed that every person should know and understand what was going on in the service, he made sure that all services would be translated into the language of the people.

Under Luther's guidance, preaching became a more prominent part of the service. He said, "The chief and greatest aim of any service is to preach and teach God's Word." He believed that God speaks through sermons. Luther himself was a great preacher, and twenty-three hundred of his sermons are still in print today.

Another change Luther made was in the use of music. He wanted all the worshipers to sing God's praises. To this end, in 1524, he published a collection of hymns. His most famous hymn, "A Mighty Fortress Is Our God," is known and loved by Christians everywhere. An African in Tanganyika once said of Luther, "He must have been a powerful man; one can feel it in his hymns."

Many parts of the service, however, were not changed. Today your church still uses pre-Lutheran songs, such as the Gloria Patri, the Kyrie, and the Gloria in Excelsis; and pre-Lutheran prayers, such as the collects. These have been elements of Christian worship since very early times. Some reformers, in other countries, removed them from worship saying that they wanted nothing at all to remind them of the old church. But Luther saw many valuable things in the old church, and it had never been his intention to start a new one. He wanted to purify the old church, to reform it. His whole purpose was to direct the church to the Bible that it might serve Jesus Christ and call all people to a faith in him.

new ways of christian living

In his preaching and writing, Luther tried to help people see what Christian living really means. No one justifies himself before God by what he does; he cannot bribe God into saving him by doing good deeds. He is in a right relationship with God only if he trusts in what Jesus Christ has done for him. Therefore, the Christian life is nothing more than living a Christlike life out of love and thanksgiving and gratitude. You don't go to church to impress God with your holiness or because you think he will punish you if you don't attend. You go to church to worship God because you know he has reached down into your life and has given you his forgiveness, his help, and his love.

The old idea, that the best way of serving God is through such spiritual exercises as prayer, masses, and vigils, was too narrow. There is no division between spiritual and secular parts of life. All of life belongs to God. As a matter of fact, he first serves us through worship and prayer before we serve him in this way. Most of all, he wants us to serve him by helping our neighbors. Luther's comment, "I will give myself as a little Christ to my neighbor as Christ gave himself for me," is worth memorizing. This is the essence of Christian living.

The old idea that priests had a favored position with God could not be true. Didn't Jesus teach everyone the Lord's Prayer? Didn't John say that "whoever believes in him should not perish but have everlasting life"? All Christians are, therefore, equal before the God of love. No one is especially favored; no one is greater than another. Luther carried this idea a step further to say that all Christians are priests of God, privileged to come to him directly, seeking forgiveness and help in prayer, and also obligated to witness to their fellowmen by leading a holy life. Luther and the other reformers believed in having ministers of the gospel, but these men were set apart only in terms of their specialized service—they held no favored position with God. If all men were equal before God, then all human work was sacred.

luther's marriage and home

Luther challenged the church in another way. He was convinced that it was no holier to remain unmarried than to marry. After all, Jesus himself blessed marriage as God's plan for the world. The family is the building block of society and the church. In support

of his belief, Luther thought he should set an example, and in June, 1525, he married a former nun, Katharine von Bora. They lived happily together in the "Black Cloister," formerly a part of the Augustinian monastery in Wittenberg. In time their daughters and sons made the big, high-ceilinged rooms ring with noise and laughter. The Luthers were a friendly family, having guests so often that Katie never knew how many people would be at the dinner table. Luther was always inviting people to share his hospitality. Meals in the Luther's home were high spots in the day. Along with the happy-hearted fellowship there were serious moments, too, when Luther taught his family and guests the truths of God's Word. Luther's *Table Talk* is a record of many of the fascinating statements he made on these occasions.

the catechisms

Luther continued to teach and preach. As he traveled about the countryside, he saw that superstition and ignorance still prevailed among many of the people. They seemed to have no knowledge of Christian doctrine. Luther realized that more Christian education and instruction was needed, and that the people themselves wanted some guide for understanding Christian truths. To meet this need, Luther prepared two books which would help the people to understand the Christian faith. They were titled the *Large* and *Small Catechisms*, and were published in 1529.

The *Large Catechism* was intended for pastors and adults. The *Small Catechism* was intended for children, and Luther expected that it would be studied in the home under the guidance of parents. Both books were based on Roman catechisms offering interpretations of the Ten Commandments, the Apostles' Creed and the Lord's Prayer. Luther added sections on the two sacraments, Baptism and Holy Communion, as well as some other items.

after frederick's death

One of the surprising things in Martin Luther's story is the large amount of freedom he had. As a man living under the ban of both the church and the emperor, you might expect that he would have been put to death, or at the very least hindered in his work.

In a sense, he made his own freedom by his determination, courage, and faith. He was not easily silenced or frightened. Another reason is that, after the Diet of Worms, Charles V was busy with other problems in the various sections of his huge empire. Duke Frederick, who had arranged for Luther to be taken to the Wartburg Castle, also protected him when he returned to Wittenberg. By the time Frederick died in 1525, other electors in several German provinces had become friendly to Luther and his ideas and were willing to protect him.

In 1526, at the Diet of Speyer, it was agreed that each prince was free to determine the religious affairs of his territory "as he would have to answer to God and the emperor."

Three years later, in another diet at Speyer, the Roman Catholic leaders were stronger. They forced repeal of the decision of 1526 and adopted stern measures unfavorable to the "heretics," as the followers of Luther were then called. Those who followed Luther's teachings protested against being forbidden to worship as they thought God wanted them to. They said, "We fear God's wrath more than we fear the emperor's ban." It was this protest which earned for the electors and princes the name "Protestant."

Finally, in 1530, Charles V was free enough from other responsibilities to return to Germany. He resolved to do something definite about the Lutheran heresy and settle it once and for all.

27

YOUR LUTHERAN HERITAGE

If you look at a map of the Holy Roman Empire in the sixteenth century, you can easily see why Charles V got involved in so many other matters besides deciding what to do about Luther. In addition to being king of Spain, Charles was emperor of a territory that included modern-day Austria, Germany, Czechoslovakia, Belgium, Holland, Luxembourg, and Switzerland—as well as parts of France, Italy, and Poland. Not only were there many internal problems connected with ruling so large an empire, but this was a time of war. The Turks were swarming out of eastern Europe like a plague of locusts and were threatening to overrun the continent. Charles V was making every effort to keep his empire strong and united in order to hold back the Turks.

TO READ AND THINK ABOUT

Isaiah 64:6-7   Our Unrighteous Righteousness
1 Peter 2:24-25   Healed
Isaiah 1:18-20   God Promises Forgiveness of Sins
John 3:31-36   Belief and Eternal Life
1 Peter 2:9-10   This You Are in Christ
Romans 10:5-13   Believe and Confess
Revelation 21:1-4   Grace and Blessings

---

the diet at augsburg

When Charles V returned to Germany in 1530, he was at the height of his power. For the purpose of achieving some sort of settlement of the religious difficulties, he called for a diet to meet at Augsburg. The day after his arrival in Augsburg, there was a procession, ablaze with color as each elector marched in full ceremonial dress to the cathedral. Within the cathedral, the emperor and all the dignitaries knelt at the high altar—all, that is, but two. The Saxon Elector John (the successor of Frederick the Wise) and Philip of Hesse refused to submit to a form of worship they believed wrong.

The next day, the Emperor summoned the Lutheran princes—among them John, Philip, and George, the Margrave of Brandenburg. He demanded that they stop Lutheran ministers from preaching in Augsburg. They refused, and the Margrave of Brandenburg stepped forward and declared, "Before I let anyone take from me the Word of God and ask me to deny my God, I will kneel and let him strike off my head."

Despite their outright defiance of his commands, the emperor gave the Lutheran princes an opportunity to present their case publicly. Luther could not be present to appear for them, since he was still technically an outlaw and had not been granted safe conduct to the meeting. But he stayed at the nearby castle of Coburg, studying the reports of the sessions and offering suggestions.

Although they did not have Luther himself, the Lutheran princes did have with them Luther's close friend Philipp Melanchthon, a renowned scholar and a professor at Wittenberg. The princes, in anticipation of an opportunity to present their case, had been working for many months to draft a document explaining their position. Melanchthon did the actual writing of this document, which was called the *Augsburg Confession*.

It took two hours to read the *Augsburg Confession* to the emperor and the members of the diet on June 25. On the document were the signatures of five princes and the representatives of two free cities. Later, representatives of four other free cities added their signatures.

More negotiations followed, and more attempts to talk the Lutherans into giving up their stubborn insistence on their rights. Finally, realizing the futility of further discussion, the emperor resorted to force. He gave the signers until the following April to change their minds and forsake the heresy. If they refused, there would be open warfare. For the emperor, the diet had been a failure.

However, the Diet of Augsburg was a success for the Lutherans. The believers in Luther's teachings had united and gained a common statement of their faith. The *Augsburg Confession* has become (along with the *Small Catechism*) the major statement of what the Lutheran church believes. June 25, 1530, can really be considered the day the Lutheran church came into its own. It had proved too strong to be either ignored or crushed. Soon afterwards, the emperor reluctantly granted the Lutherans freedom of worship.

luther's later years

As the years went by, Luther continued to preach, teach, and write. He still had his courage and his power with words. But many bouts with illness took their toll on both his body and spirit. At times he grew quite intolerant of his critics. He was quick at name-calling; he lashed out at his enemies with tongue and pen. There were times when he was depressed and downcast. Then Katie, his good wife, had to remind him to trust his Lord.

Luther called himself "a child and a pupil" of the good news of salvation in Jesus Christ. Once he wrote, "Christ has made the children our teachers. I am chagrined that although I am ever so much a doctor, I still have to go to the same school with Hans and Magdalena (Luther's children). . . ."

Death came to Luther on February 18, 1546. He had gone to Eisleben to help settle a legal quarrel. His arbitration was successful, and finally, on February 17, an agreement was signed. That night Luther complained of faintness and pressure around his heart. At 2 A.M. his friends were roused with the news that Luther had taken a turn for the worse. One of them said to him, "Reverend father, will you stand steadfast by Christ and the doctrine you have preached?" The dying Luther whispered, "Yes."

Four days later, Luther was interred in the Castle Church of Wittenberg. On the door of this same church, twenty-nine years earlier, he had nailed his Ninety-five Theses. And although he was gone, the church that bore his name grew stronger daily as it dedicated itself to carrying on the work that he had begun.

luther and you

Today your church still gladly bears the name of Luther. It does this because Luther made the church once more the church of Jesus Christ. We believe that Luther was right when he insisted that the Bible is the sole authority for all that is taught and believed in the Christian church.

As Lutherans, we do not believe that we must climb a ladder of good works, prayers, and sacrifices to reach God; nor do we believe that God loves us only when we are doing things to prove our loyalty, such as giving up candy for Lent. A man's Christian faith is not measured by how good he appears to be.

Instead, as Lutherans, we believe that we are Christians through faith in Jesus Christ. This faith keeps us aware of God's love for us. Even when we sin he still loves us. It's wonderful to have a God who cares, and to know that although he does not like what you are doing when you sin, he still likes you and sees all the possibilities of your becoming a new person in Christ. By faith, you know that he still wants you to be with him and follow him.

As a Lutheran, you see the things of this world as gifts of God's love to you. These things can be used selfishly. When they are misused this way, they become evil. On the other hand, they can be used in the service of God and fellowmen, in love. Then they are being used as God wants them to be used.

Naturally we don't worship Luther as a saint; he was far from perfect. No man but Christ was ever perfect. But we honor Luther for his great contributions to the church. We are thankful that God used him to cleanse the church. We remember him because he called the church back to the Bible, particularly to the New Testament, where men can know the real truths of God in Christ.

171

IHC

Part Eight

The New Life in Christ

28

THE POWER OF LOVE

Paul says that in Baptism you are buried into the death of Christ so that as Christ was raised from death so you, too, might "walk in newness of life" (Romans 6:4). Paul means that being baptized is like drowning our sin and selfishness. We are, therefore, brought into a warm, unique relationship with God by his invitation. Listen to Paul again: "But you were washed (baptized), you were sanctified (made holy), you were justified (made right with God) in the name of the Lord Jesus Christ and in the Spirit of our God" (1 Corinthians 6:11). As Christians we are privileged to have a new life in Christ.

TO READ AND THINK ABOUT

Psalm 63:1-4   God's Love Is Better than Life
Psalm 136   His Steadfast Love
John 14:18-24   Showing Our Love for Christ
1 Corinthians 13   A Hymn of Love
1 John 4:7-16   God Is Love
1 John 5:1-5   Love and the Commandments
1 Thessalonians 3:11-13   Abound in Love

---

the measure of a christian

By Baptism you became a Christian. You remain a Christian through faith in Jesus Christ. Each day as you confess Jesus Christ to be your Lord, believing that he redeems and saves you, you bear the name of Christ well.

Every day you have many decisions to make. Some are very critical choices, others are relatively insignificant. But the most important is that every day you have to decide whether or not you are going to conduct yourself as a Christian.

Pupils in a church school class were once asked to write a brief statement describing Christianity. One girl wrote, "Christianity is thinking things through with Christ in mind." This definition doesn't describe the whole nature of Christianity, but it does emphasize a very important point. What a difference it makes to think things through with Christ!

As a Christian, you don't rely on snap judgments or on the way you feel when you are faced with making the right choice. You pray and seek Jesus' guidance, asking him to help you so you won't decide selfishly. Whatever you do, you want your actions to reflect your love of God and your desire to let that love shine through all your associations with your fellowmen.

concern for others

During the American Civil War, the Union and Confederate forces fought for several bloody hours on a little farm in Kentucky. The tenants of the farm ordered their young son to stay in the cellar for safety. But he couldn't sit still in the darkness while the roar of cannons and the whistle of bullets could be heard outside. He just had to see the battle for himself.

Slipping out of the house, the boy made his way carefully through the woods to the back pastures, where the sounds of fighting seemed the loudest. Billowing smoke clouds, flashes of ugly red, and the deafening rumble of guns made him think that he was in another world. For a split second, he thought of running back to the protection of the shelter. But he felt that maybe he could do something to help, so he went on.

Suddenly he came to a group of wounded men. Some were screaming with pain; others lay dully on the ground, blood streaming from their wounds. A Union officer, obviously a doctor, was moving swiftly from man to man, trying to give first-aid treatment. It didn't seem to matter whether a wounded soldier wore blue or gray, the doctor tried to help each man. As the doctor paused to wipe away the streaming perspiration from his dirty face, he saw the boy standing there at the edge of the field, transfixed with wonder, fear, and sympathy.

"Don't just stand there, boy," bellowed the doctor, "come and give me a hand."

Slowly the boy inched his way forward to the doctor's side. Before them was a Confederate cavalryman, scarcely more than a boy himself. His right leg was oddly twisted and, where the doctor had cut his boot away, there was a sickening sight of shattered bone and muscle. "Help me get him bandaged," ordered the doctor as he knelt at the soldier's side.

Gulping, the boy reached out to touch the injured leg with a quivering hand. As he did, he looked straight into the eyes of the cavalryman. He saw pain in those eyes; and he also saw appreciation and thankfulness for help. Without a word and with a steadied, unhesitating hand, the boy bent to his task, gently removing bits of clothing and boot from the wound so the doctor could bandage it up.

For over twelve hours, the boy worked alongside the doctor, forgetting himself, forgetting time, forgetting the horrible sights and smells, knowing only that here were men who needed help desperately. What was it that made him able to do it? You could only call it love, a feeling of concern and compassion for someone else. Love gives people power to do many things that they might not like to do or even want to do.

the great resource of love

In your geography classes, you have learned about the great natural resources of your country. There is oil, so valuable it is called "black gold," locked in the layers of shale; there is uranium ore; there is coal—to name only a few. Natural resources help make a nation great. By using them well, the people of a nation can build a better life for themselves. God, who put resources into the land, also put resources of power in human beings to help them live the new life in Christ. One of the greatest of these is the ability to love.

Love is the only cure for selfishness. Love enables a person to put aside thoughts about himself and to be more concerned about the needs and rights of others. How else could you explain the way parents do all they can for a baby? How else could you explain the act of a girl in Wisconsin who rushed into the path of a speeding car in order to push her little brother on his tricycle out of the way?

Paul wrote a whole chapter describing the power of love in his First Letter to the Corinthians. His words are worth memorizing; they are magnificent. In *The New Testament in Modern English*, J. B. Phillips translates the eighth verse this way: "Love knows no limit to its endurance, no end to its trust, no fading of its hope; it can outlast anything. It is, in fact, the one thing that still stands when all else has fallen."

Keep the power of love in mind whenever you think about the Ten Commandments. Remember that Jesus said the two greatest commandments were to love God and to love your neighbor. "On these two commandments," he said, "depend all the law . . ." (Matthew 22:40). The reason you need to think about love is that, without it, often you may feel helpless before God's laws.

There are the Commandments, standing so perfect and pure before you like a mountain. The kind of life that comes from unfailing obedience to them may seem so far away from the kind of life you live from day to day that you feel hopeless. Maybe you try to keep God's laws but realize with shame how often you fail. Or maybe you try to concentrate on one part of your life, perfecting that according to God's directions, only to discover that you are falling down somewhere else. You soon discover that you can't, no matter how hard you try, create the perfect life for yourself. That's why you and other worshipers pray together a prayer of repentance at the very beginning of The Service: "Almighty God, our Maker and Redeemer, we poor sinners confess unto thee, that we are by nature sinful and unclean, and that we have sinned against thee by thought, word, and deed. . . ."

God knows that you are unable to obey his Commandments by your own strength. So he gives you extra power, especially the power of love. You see, love helps in two ways. It gives purpose and direction to what you do as well as helping you do it.

love at work

For some people, calisthenics is a horrible word. They don't like to do exercises just for the sake of doing exercises. Look at the expressions on the faces of your friends in gym class when they are doing pushups or deep knee bends. Listen to them groan and complain.

But go out on the football field and watch the team doing calisthenics at a practice session. They have much more rigorous exercises to do, yet they don't seem to mind. What's the difference? The football players know that doing the exercises will help them

play well. They really want to be in shape; they want the team to win. Whether or not they like calisthenics isn't really important. But for people in a gym class who have no goal for their exercises, putting their bodies through the paces doesn't seem to count for anything.

Take another illustration. Maybe your parents have a whole list of chores they expect you to do around the house. It may seem like a terrible burden—cut the grass, rake the leaves, wash the dishes, take out the garbage. If you look at these jobs as limits to your freedom, you will suffer. If your parents insist strongly enough, you will do as you are told, but you'll still be grumbling and complaining under your breath. Maybe you'll look for every way possible to cut corners and get out of doing as much work as you can.

But suppose, on the other hand, that you look upon household tasks as a way of helping your parents. You love them. You like your home. You want to do things to make them happy and take some of the work of running the house from their shoulders. They may still tell you that you have to shovel snow, but you do it not because it was an order but because you feel it is your responsibility. Then one day maybe you even shovel snow without being told; you want to surprise them. You go to work with enthusiasm; the words of appreciation you get are worth all the work. Love has taken the

sting out of obedience. Love makes you want to discipline yourself. Love has given you a goal.

All the way through the Commandments, God is asking us to put love to work. When you love God, you'll do everything you can to make him happy; when you love other people you'll use every chance you get to help them.

love is freedom

When you learn how to love, you learn the secret of freedom. Your country prides itself on being a free nation. Yet there are a great many laws to obey. The men who drew them up knew that laws are necessary in order to preserve human liberty. A man is truly free not when he has no rules or laws to obey, but when he willingly accepts and obeys laws protecting the freedoms of others.

Paul says that when we accept the gospel of God's love, which Jesus Christ made clear to us, we are free from the burden of God's Law. This may seem to say that the Ten Commandments no longer apply to us when we become Christians, but that is not what Paul means at all.

He means that we can be free from feeling that obedience is a burden. He is saying that when we live with love in our hearts, God's laws are not heavy chains to carry. Only when we sin, when we forget to love, do God's laws become a club to force us to do what the needs of others require us to do. As disciples of Christ, we obey God's laws and follow his directions gladly because the love of God has given purpose to our lives. God's love for us has made such a deep impression that we want to love in return.

we love because he first loved us

Love is contagious. That's what John means when he writes, "We love, because he first loved us" (1 John 4:19). The most striking thing about the love of God is that he loves us, each of us, with all our faults and sins. He sees in us all the good things that we are capable of doing, the fine persons we are capable of becoming. Only a fool would turn down a love like that.

The perfect way to see God's love in action is to look at Jesus. We have talked about this before, but it is worth underscoring many times. When you read in the Gospels of the way Jesus made love real—from healing a sick child to forgiving his enemies from the cross—you begin to realize something of the power of that love.

Augustus Saint-Gaudens, one famous Irish-American sculptor, came to realize this in a very dramatic way. Once, Saint-Gaudens was commissioned to do a statue of Phillips Brooks, to be placed outside Trinity Episcopal Church in Boston. Dr. Brooks had been rector of the church for many years and had been well loved by his congregation as an outstanding preacher and pastor. (You may know that Phillips Brooks wrote the familiar Christmas hymn "O Little Town of Bethlehem.")

In order to do the sculpture, Saint-Gaudens did a lot of research on Brooks's background and personality. The sculptor felt that he should study the New Testament to see what had made Brooks the man he was. After reading and rereading the Gospels, Saint-Gaudens was struck with the power and love of Christ. He said, "This man, Jesus, can have me. He can have all of me if he wants me."

When the time came for the statue to be unveiled, the people watching on the sidewalk beside Trinity Church were amazed to see two figures of stone instead of one. There was Phillips Brooks, standing erect, his arm outstretched as though he were preaching; and there behind him, with his hand on Brooks's shoulder, stood the figure of Christ.

Saint-Gaudens had succeeded in finding what had made Brooks the man he was. He had realized the power of Christ's love and he had shown it in his sculpture.

love is the way God lives in us

So great, so strong, so all-encompassing is God's love that one of the best ways we can try to describe it, and its influence on our lives is to say that God *is* love. This is true whether you speak of God the Father, God the Son Jesus Christ, or God the Holy Spirit. Everything about God is love. This is a very important fact to remember. It means:

1. *That God by his love lives within us.*
   John says, "So have we come to know and trust the love God has for us. God *is* love, and the man whose life is lived in love does, in fact, live in God, and God does, in fact, live in him" (1 John 4:16, Phillips' translation).
2. *That we show our love for God by obeying his commandments.*
   John says, "For loving God means obeying his commands, and these commands of his are not burdensome, for God's 'heredity' within us will always conquer the world outside us. In fact, this faith of ours is the only way in which the world has been conquered" (1 John 5:3-4, Phillips' translation).

God wants more than anything else to release the power of love in your life. He wants to live so closely with you that you will spend your life together and his commandments will be a description of the way your life flows on from day to day, on through the eternal life to come.

29
FORGIVENESS

Three of the most loving and most welcome words in the English language are "I forgive you." When someone you have accidentally or intentionally hurt forgives you, your actions—which could have built a wall between you and that person—are forgotten. Forgiveness gives you a chance to start all over again.

TO READ AND THINK ABOUT
Psalm 32:1-5   Blessed Is the Forgiven Person
Psalm 130:1-4   There Is Forgiveness
Luke 7:36-50   Jesus Forgives a Woman
Matthew 26:26-29   The Last Supper
1 John 1:5-10   God Is Faithful and Just
Colossians 1:11-14   Forgiveness in Christ
Matthew 6:9-15   Prayer for Forgiveness

If there were no such thing as forgiveness, life would be miserable. You would have a hard time living comfortably at home. Think of the many times you have to ask your parents and other members of your family to overlook your conduct. You would also have a hard time getting along with people outside your home. You and your friends have to forgive each other many times over if you are going to remain friends.

If there were no forgiveness, your relationship with God would be impossible. Long ago, you would have cut him out of your life by your thoughts, words, or deeds.

Fortunately for us, anyone can offer forgiveness; and anyone can receive it. And what is even more important than the forgiveness of our family and friends is the forgiveness of God. Forgiveness is part of God's love. Whenever God comes to us through his Word, through Jesus, through his church, through the lives of Christian people, he comes telling us that he is willing to forgive our sins.

a resource for christian living

Forgiveness is a great resource that God gives to us for our daily living as Christians. When we look at ourselves honestly and see our failures to obey the Commandments, when we become aware of how often we do not love God with all our hearts and our fellowmen as ourselves, then we can only ask God's forgiveness. There is nothing else that we can do. We can't make up for our actions; we can't right the wrongs or heal the hurts. We have to depend on God's love. And he never fails us.

Forgiveness was at the very heart of Jesus' ministry. He came into the lives of a corrupt public official, a woman taken in adultery, a sick man burdened as much with a guilty conscience as with his physical disease—and he forgave them all. Because of his forgiveness, these and many others became new people, able to hold their heads high and walk without shame.

Where would Paul, the great Christian missionary, have been if God had not forgiven him for ordering the murders of innocent Christians? God changed Paul and helped him do great things.

As part of the prayer we should use to talk to God our Father, Jesus taught us to say, "Forgive us our trespasses as we forgive those who trespass against us." He wanted us never to forget the great importance of forgiveness both in our relations with God and in our relations with our fellowmen. Forgiveness brings man and God together again after sin has broken their close relationship. Forgiveness is also what enables people to live with one another in peace and contentment.

good manners

As you grow up, you learn a lot about good manners. Manners are the name we give to courteous conduct toward others. They don't include only the small, mechanical rules—like putting the knife on a certain side of the dinner plate, or a boy's walking on the curb side of a girl when he's going along the street. The most important kinds of manners are the kinds that reflect your concern for the rights and the happiness of others. If you accidentally step on someone's foot in a crowded room, you say, "I beg your pardon," or "Please excuse me," or "I'm sorry." You have even learned to ask forgiveness if you walk in front of another person or interrupt his conversation. Manners, after all, are a mark of kindness and thoughtfulness, especially when we use them to show that we don't want to offend or harm anyone—or that we are sorry for having done so.

In this sense, it is good manners for a Christian to ask God's forgiveness as soon as he knows that he has offended God. Suppose you realize that you have broken one of the Commandments. In that flash of awareness, speak a private word to God; confess your weakness; ask his help. No matter where you are or what you are doing, you can afford to spend a few moments in prayer.

Suppose you heard some juicy gossip about what Bill did after the Sadie Hawkins dance. You are about to tell the gang about it, when you get a sort of guilty feeling about doing so. When this happens, stop right there and ask God's forgiveness mentally. After you have, it will be practically impossible for you to continue with the story. More likely, you will think of something good to say about Bill. Why ask God's forgiveness instead of Bill's? Because if you hurt Bill, you are hurting God, too. By being unkind, you are not obeying his Commandments.

Suppose you are wrestling with the temptation to do something that you know is wrong. Stop; ask God to forgive your willingness to even consider going against his will for your life. You will be amazed at the added strength you will have to resist the temptation no matter how powerful it seemed before. God's forgiveness sends greater power for good into our lives.

Of course, seeking God's forgiveness is more than simply having good manners. You can't live in fellowship with God without forgiveness.

accepting forgiveness

When Andrew Jackson was President of the United States, he was involved in a very peculiar situation. He had written out a full pardon for a man named George Wilson, who had been sentenced

to death and was now in a Pennsylvania prison waiting for his execution. Wilson had been convicted of robbing the U.S. mails and of murder, for which the court had sentenced him to hang. Jackson's pardon, of course, would make Wilson a free man.

But for some reason, Wilson refused to accept the pardon. What's more, he even argued that unless he did accept it, it wasn't a pardon at all. Wilson's action threw the federal government into confusion. It seemed a minor, technical problem of law, but the best legal minds in Washington could not seem to decide whether or not Wilson was right. Finally, Jackson turned the matter over to the Supreme Court.

After long deliberation with his colleagues, Chief Justice John Marshall reported the court's decision: "A pardon is a paper, the value of which depends upon its acceptance by the person implicated. It is hardly supposed that one under sentence of death would refuse to accept a pardon, but if it is refused, it is no pardon. George Wilson must be hanged."

In 1829, according to the due process of law, Wilson was executed. The nation's newspapers found the story hard to believe. It seemed incredible that a man could have deliberately refused to accept an offer of forgiveness, that he could have chosen instead to die.

Forgiveness is only forgiveness when it is accepted. If you believe that God has forgiven you when you have asked him, then you have to act like a forgiven person. Unless you forgive yourself, you have not accepted God's forgiveness. Some people make themselves miserable by continuing to blame themselves for things they did long ago, even though they have been forgiven.

what forgiveness is

Forgiveness is really a kind of miracle. The whole idea of forgiveness comes from God. It is a way of blotting out the past as though it had never happened, at least as far as our guilt is concerned. John puts it this way, "If we confess our sins, he is faithful and just, and will forgive our sins and cleanse us from all unrighteousness" (1 John 1:9).

Sin is like making a lot of chalk marks on a clean chalkboard; forgiveness is like taking an eraser and wiping them away. God wipes away our sins for us because he loves us. To show us this loving forgiveness, he gave us Jesus so that whoever believes in Jesus as his Lord can find complete forgiveness. (Reread John 3:16-17.)

The two sacraments, Baptism and Holy Communion, both remind us of God's forgiveness. The water of Baptism symbolizes the way God's love washes sin away. The bread and wine of Communion remind us that, by giving himself in the sacrifice of the cross, Jesus has provided a way of forgiving our sins each day and bringing us into "communion" or fellowship with God as though we had never sinned at all. Through the medium of the bread and wine we receive that forgiveness Christ won for us and enter into a close relationship with our Savior. Just as your parents' forgiveness makes you feel that you are once more part of the family circle, so God's forgiveness draws you back into the close relationship you should have with him as his son.

a word of caution

Talking about forgiveness makes it seem easy to sin. It sounds as if, no matter what you do, God will remove your guilt. This is true—provided you are sorry for your sins and are willing to accept his forgiveness. But you still have to bear whatever penalty your sin has caused. It would be silly to think that you could break God's Commandments any time you wanted to as long as you asked his pardon.

Bruce was very sorry when he heaved a baseball through the supermarket window. He was really throwing to Joey Adams at second base on the ball diamond behind the store. But his throw went wild. The manager of the store listened to Bruce's story and forgave him. He realized that the broken window was an accident, so he didn't call the police. But he did say that Bruce would have to bring him money every week out of his allowance until the window was paid for. Bruce went home angry; he stomped into the house and complained bitterly to his father. To his surprise, his father said that the manager was right. "It's your responsibility, Bruce," he said, "to make up as best you can for what you have done."

Annette lost her temper in an argument with her sister. The girls had been cutting out material for skirts for themselves. Neither knew what started the battle. But Annette got so angry that she threw a pair of scissors at her sister. To her horror, the blades slashed into Jean's arm. Annette felt terrible; she did everything she could to let her sister know how sorry she was. Jean forgave her and, after her arm was bandaged, she never mentioned the incident again. Annette was so ashamed of her action that she asked God's forgiveness, too. We are sure that God also forgave her. But Jean will have a long scar on her arm as long as she lives. And every time Annette sees that scar, she remembers what anger can do.

Both Bruce and Annette are forgiven people, yet they both have to pay the penalty for their actions. They are never again going to be quite the same as they were before the incidents happened.

forgiveness is power

Forgiveness is power God releases in your life to give you a second chance. Without forgiveness, life would be unbearable, wouldn't it? Remember this great gift of God which he offers to you when you need it. Of course, it would be much better if we learned to live by love so that we would not need to be forgiven so often. If we let God take over more and more of our lives this will happen.

30

LIVING WITH A THANKFUL HEART

Along with love and forgiveness, God gives us a third great resource to help us live the new life in Christ—thankfulness. Being thankful is being appreciative of all that God has done for you. When you feel thankful for God's gifts, you will take care of them and use them wisely.

TO READ AND THINK ABOUT
Psalm 106:1-3   Give Thanks to the Lord
Ephesians 5:15-20   Always Give Thanks
1 Thessalonians 5:12-22   Thanksgiving Is the Will of God
1 Timothy 2:1-4   Thanksgiving for Men
Romans 14:5-9   Thanksgiving for Honor
Philippians 4:4-7   Thanksgiving in Prayer
Colossians 2:6-7   Abounding in Thanksgiving

Look at the difference between the Smiths and the Joneses. Both families like to go camping in the summertime; both generally go to a national park. The Smiths like to camp because they love nature and enjoy living close to it. After they have left their camp site and gone home, you would hardly know that they had been there. The ashes of the fire are scattered and soaked with water, the grounds are clean and neat, all rubbish is gone. The Joneses, on the other hand, look upon camping as a cheap vacation. They are in the woods to have a good time and they do what they want to do. When they leave for home, the fire is still burning with some green branches chopped off a living tree. Bottles and trash are every-where. On the picnic table may be a jar of wild flowers pulled from a meadow, along with some birds' nests complete with eggs. On nearby trees, you may find the children's initials carved in the bark. Of course, we are deliberately drawing an extreme picture here. But it is easy to see which family really appreciates having an oppor-tunity to share the beauties and wonders of nature. They use them wisely and leave them intact for others to enjoy.

Jesus and the lepers

How many people are thankful for God's gracious gifts? There are no statistics to give us an answer. If you look at the ten lepers that Jesus healed on one occasion, you may come to the conclusion that only one out of ten people is grateful.

Leprosy is a vile disease. Because it was so contagious, lepers in biblical times had to live in total isolation. They were forced to leave their homes and live in caves outside their villages. Moreover, they had to call out "Unclean!" when anyone came nearby so that whoever was passing would know they were there and be able to avoid them. Imagine what it must be like to have a dread disease for which there is no known cure, to see your flesh slowly rotting away. If you had a disease like that and someone helped you, you would probably feel so thankful that you could hardly do enough to show your gratitude.

Yet only one of the ten men Jesus healed came back to give thanks. The other nine had gone their way. (Read the story in Luke 17:12-19.) Perhaps some of the others were thankful, too, but they kept silent about it.

The leper who thanked Jesus had really received more than just the gift of healing; he now had the power of a thankful heart. The healing of his disease-ridden body had changed his life; his feeling of thankfulness would make his new life count for something.

what thankful living can do for you

Why make such a big case for thankfulness? Because if you feel grateful for what you have, your whole attitude toward life is affected.

Take the matter of money. No matter how little or how much you have, you will be unhappy unless you are thankful for it. You may think that you deserve a higher allowance from your parents or that you should be better paid for the odd jobs you do. But when you think this way, the satisfaction in having money soon turns sour; you don't even enjoy spending it because you think you could be spending more. And the very thought of giving any of your precious money *away*, even to someone who needs it, makes you shudder. You may feel resentful that your church asks you for an offering to help carry on its work; you may look the other way when you see a blind beggar holding out his tin cup.

The Jews of the Old Testament world believed in tithing, giving God a tenth of all their possessions. They were supposed to do this out of gratitude to God for all the rich blessings he gave them. Perhaps some Jews grumbled that it wasn't fair; but others rejoiced in being able to share what they had with God.

187

The writers of the New Testament were not so much concerned with the legal idea of giving a tenth as they were with the idea of gratitude. A person who truly appreciates his possessions not only takes good care of them but also shares them gladly with others. This is the whole idea of stewardship.

All of man's money is to be used for the glory of God. The money a father uses to provide for his family is just as much a part of good stewardship as the taxes he pays or what he gives beyond that to help others.

According to this view, Christians do not give because they have to; they give because they want to give. Jesus praised the poor widow in the Temple who put only a few copper coins into the offering box. He knew that many wealthy people gave only what they wouldn't miss, but that this woman needed every penny to get along. Yet she was thankful for what she had, and she was glad to share it. (Read the story in Mark 12:41-44.)

Thankful living, as far as money is concerned, means that you control your money instead of letting it control you. Having money, then, does not just enable you to buy things for your own pleasure; it offers you an opportunity to show your thankfulness by helping others. The percentage that you give to church or charity is entirely up to you—it really depends a lot on how thankful you feel.

Another place where thankful Christian living should play an important part is in your home. Gratitude can make all the difference in the world between being happy and unhappy. If only for the purely selfish reason of wanting a contented home life, it is smart to appreciate what your parents do for you. If you do not seem grateful for the many things they give you, but keep demanding more and more of them, you can make your home life pretty miserable—both for yourself and for your parents. Shakespeare expressed a parent's point of view clearly when he wrote, "How sharper than a serpent's tooth it is to have a thankless child!"

But your gratitude is part of your home life for better reasons than selfish ones. You know that God has commanded you to honor your parents, to love them and care for them. This means to appreciate them, too. When you are thankful, you draw closer to them. You begin to realize how many sacrifices they have made on your behalf. You see how frequently they skimp on things they need in order to provide you with the good things of life. They do so gladly because they love you. And you can show your love and appreciation for this by looking around to see what you can do to please them and help them. Sometimes the best way of saying "Thank you" for a good meal is by offering to do the dishes. There is an old

saying that "actions speak louder than words." Don't forget the words, they are important, too. But they are not a substitute for actions.

gratitude in daily living

If you want to keep your friends, you are careful to let them know that you appreciate their friendship. Because you are grateful for it, you are quick to forgive their faults and willing to overlook the times they may hurt you.

Carry this feeling of gratitude over to your school. When you begin to appreciate your teachers for their willingness to teach you, your attitude toward your work changes. You come to realize how important are your studies and how lucky you are to be able to go to school and learn so much about the world in which you live. Often, people miss the real joy of learning until they graduate. Then they wish they had made better use of their opportunities for study. If you are thankful for the gift of education, you'll work hard now to get all the rich rewards of a trained mind.

Gratitude also lies behind good citizenship. The person who is grateful for his country's freedom and way of life becomes a real patriot. He is willing to do what he can to support his country. Instead of demanding that his country do more and more for him, he looks for ways in which he can help his country be an even better place in which to live. Gratitude breeds loyalty; and loyalty, sacrifice. Nathan Hale, a schoolmaster turned spy for the American colonies, could never have said those famous words, "I only regret that I have but one life to lose for my country," if he were not thankful for all that his homeland meant to him.

Take any area of life and see how much poorer your experiences are when you neglect thankfulness. Thankfulness is really the climate of your inner life which nourishes the growth of what we call Christian virtues. Things like faith, hope, love, forgiveness, self-discipline, patience—you could add a lot of others to the list—work best when they come from gratitude.

thankfulness is a way of living with God

You may have heard of Izaak Walton, who wrote the first book about fishing. Walton believed that Christianity was the greatest thing that had ever happened to the world. He commented that "God has two dwellings: one in heaven and the other in a meek and thankful heart."

"Only those are truly thankful who receive the gifts of God joyfully and rejoice in the Giver" is Luther's way of saying that our happiness because God belongs to us and we belong to him is the starting point of real thanksgiving. And the way to show this thankfulness is to live the kind of Christian life God requests of us. We can't really give him anything else. All that we have comes from God and so is already his. We can only give him praise and honor and thanks, and show that we mean it by living according to the example of Christ.

In our worship of God, we remind ourselves of all we have received from him, including the greatest gift of all, Jesus Christ. The words that Jesus spoke at the Last Supper bring this truth home to us. He took the bread from the table and shared it with his disciples, saying, "Take, eat; this is my body." He took the wine cup and passed it around, saying, "Drink of it, all of you; for this is my blood . . ." In doing this, Christ was telling us that he gives us himself, all of his holy personality, to be a part of our lives. With his presence comes his forgiveness, his strength to withstand temptations, his courage to live holy lives in love. This is a lot to be thankful for. Those who take Communion know that God is uniting himself to them through Christ. If they are really thankful, they will leave the altar determined to do all they can to make their lives worthy of God's gift.

Soon you will be participating in the Sacrament of the Altar with the rest of your congregation. If you think of it as just another church ritual you have to go through, you won't get much out of the experience. But if you think of it in terms of thanksgiving, of dedicating yourself anew to the God who gave everything he has to you, it will be one of the most meaningful experiences of your regular worship.

But you don't have to wait until you are admitted to the Lord's Table to express your thankfulness. You can live every day with a thankful heart right now. And each new experience of worship, each new experience of life itself, will bring added blessings and greater, more lasting satisfaction.

building on Christ

Jesus once told a story of two builders. One built his house upon rock, basing the foundation of his house on something solid. The rain fell; the floods came; the wind blew. But the house stood firm. It could take the storms.

The other builder built his house upon sand. When the rain fell, the floods came, and the wind blew upon this house, it tumbled to the ground. It couldn't take the storms because the foundation wasn't good (Matthew 7:24-27).

There is a similar difference between people. Some hear the words of Christ and seek to live by them. They are like the builder whose house was built upon rock. Others are indifferent to the words of Christ. They feel they can live the way they want to and can ignore Christ altogether. These are like the builder whose house had a shaky foundation and eventually collapsed.

To be a Christian is to build your life upon the solid rock of Jesus Christ. Christ has given himself to you, and as the foundation of your life, he is present to help you at all times. For your part, he asks only your willingness to live the new life in his name, both now and throughout eternity.

Note on symbols used in this book:

PAGE	TITLE	SIGNIFICANCE
8	*Alpha and Omega*	Symbol for Christ, the beginning and the end of life. Alpha and Omega are first and last letters of Greek alphabet.
32	*Hand of God*	Symbol of the presence and the will of God the Father.
53	*The Two Tablets*	Symbol for the Ten Commandments, inscribed on two stone tablets.
82	*The Root of Jesse*	Symbol for Christ. Christ's ancestry can be traced to Jesse, father of David. Therefore, the Star of David is shown with the roots. (Read Isaiah 11:1)
108	*The Fish*	Symbol for Christ. Origin of symbol is in acrostic formed by letters in Greek word for fish (Ichthus). Letters stand for: Jesus Christ, Son of God, Savior.
118	*The Chi Rho*	Symbol of Christ. These Greek letters stand for the first two letters in the name "Christ."
148	*The Lamb of God*	Symbol for Christ. The lamb was used for Jewish sacrifices. Christ offered himself as sacrifice for the sins of the world. The cross-emblazoned banner in the symbol points to the triumph of Easter.
172	*The IHS*	Symbol for Christ. These Greek letters stand for the first three letters of the name "Jesus."

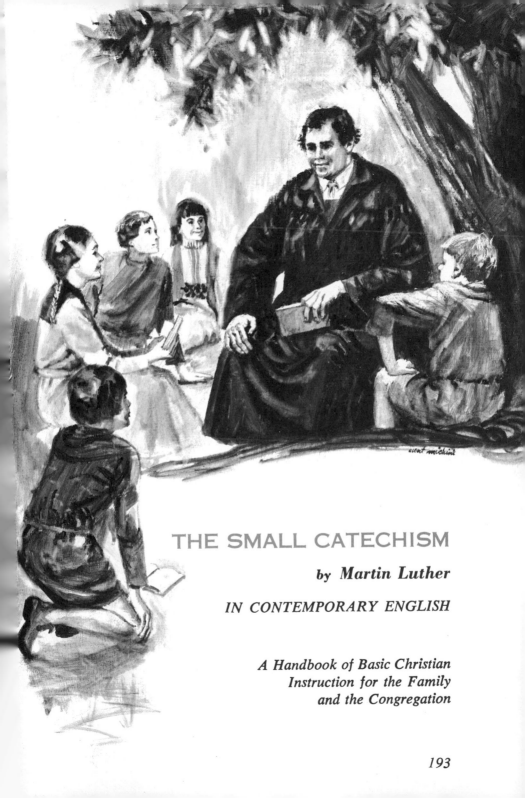

THE SMALL CATECHISM

by *Martin Luther*

IN CONTEMPORARY ENGLISH

*A Handbook of Basic Christian
Instruction for the Family
and the Congregation*

Part One

THE TEN COMMANDMENTS

I am the Lord your God.

The First Commandment

You shall have no other gods.

What does this mean for us?

We are to fear, love, and trust God above anything else.

The Second Commandment

You shall not take the name of the Lord your God in vain.

What does this mean for us?

We are to fear and love God so that we do not use his name to curse, swear, lie, or deceive, but call on him in prayer, praise, and thanksgiving.

The Third Commandment

Remember the Sabbath day, to keep it holy.

What does this mean for us?

We are to fear and love God so that we do not neglect his Word and the preaching of it, but regard it as holy and gladly hear and learn it.

The Fourth Commandment

Honor your father and your mother.

What does this mean for us?

We are to fear and love God so that we do not despise or anger our parents and others in authority, but respect, obey, love, and serve them.

The Fifth Commandment

You shall not kill.

What does this mean for us?

We are to fear and love God so that we do not hurt our neighbor in any way, but help him in all his physical needs.

The Sixth Commandment

You shall not commit adultery.

What does this mean for us?

We are to fear and love God so that in matters of sex our words and conduct are pure and honorable, and husband and wife love and respect each other.

The Seventh Commandment

You shall not steal.

What does this mean for us?

We are to fear and love God so that we do not take our neighbor's money or property, or get them in any dishonest way, but help him to improve and protect his property and means of making a living.

The Eighth Commandment

You shall not bear false witness against your neighbor.

What does this mean for us?

We are to fear and love God so that we do not betray, slander, or lie about our neighbor, but defend him, speak well of him, and explain his actions in the kindest way.

The Ninth Commandment

You shall not covet your neighbor's house.

What does this mean for us?

We are to fear and love God so that we do not desire to get our neighbor's possessions by scheming, or by pretending to have a right to them, but always help him keep what is his.

The Tenth Commandment

You shall not covet your neighbor's wife, or his manservant, or his maidservant, or his cattle, or anything that is your neighbor's

What does God say of all these Commandments?

He says: "I, the Lord your God, am a jealous God, visiting the iniquity of the fathers upon the children to the third and fourth generation of those who hate me, but showing steadfast love to thousands of those who love me and keep my commandments."

What does this mean for us?

We are to fear and love God so that we do not tempt or coax away from our neighbor his wife or his workers, but encourage them to remain loyal.

What does this mean for us?

God warns that he will punish all who break these commandments.
Therefore we are to fear his wrath and not disobey him.
But he promises grace and every blessing to all who keep these commandments.
Therefore we are to love and trust him, and gladly do what he commands.

Part Two
THE APOSTLES' CREED

The First Article

I believe in God the Father almighty, Maker of heaven and earth.

What does this mean?

I believe that God has created me and all that exists.
He has given me and still preserves my body and soul with all their powers.

He provides me with food and clothing, home and family, daily work, and all I need from day to day.

God also protects me in time of danger and guards me from every evil.

All this he does out of fatherly and divine goodness and mercy, though I do not deserve it.
Therefore I surely ought to thank and praise, serve and obey him.

This is most certainly true.

The Second Article

And in Jesus Christ his only Son, our Lord; who was conceived by the Holy Ghost, born of the Virgin Mary; suffered under Pontius Pilate, was crucified, dead, and buried; he descended into hell; the third day he rose again from the dead; he ascended into heaven, and sitteth on the right hand of God the Father almighty; from thence he shall come to judge the quick and the dead.

What does this mean?

I believe that Jesus Christ—true God, Son of the Father from eternity, and true man, born of the Virgin Mary—is my Lord.

He has redeemed me, a lost and condemned person, saved me at great cost from sin, death, and the power of the devil—not with silver or gold, but with his holy and precious blood and his innocent suffering and death.

All this he has done that I may be his own, live under him in his kingdom, and serve him in everlasting righteousness, innocence, and blessedness, just as he is risen from the dead and lives and rules eternally.

This is most certainly true.

The Third Article

*I believe in the Holy Ghost;
the holy Christian church,
the communion of saints;
the forgiveness of sins; the
resurrection of the body;
and the life everlasting.
Amen.*

What does this mean?

I believe that I cannot by my
own understanding or effort
believe in Jesus Christ my
Lord, or come to him.
But the Holy Spirit has called
me through the gospel,
enlightened me with his gifts,
and sanctified and kept me in
true faith.

In the same way he calls,
gathers, enlightens, and
sanctifies the whole Christian
church on earth, and keeps
it united with Jesus Christ in
the one true faith.

In this Christian church day
after day he fully forgives my
sins and the sins of all
believers.
On the last day he will raise
me and all the dead and give
me and all believers in Christ
eternal life.

This is most certainly true.

Part Three
THE LORD'S PRAYER

The Introduction

*Our Father who art in
heaven.*

What does this mean?

Here God encourages us to
believe that he is truly our
Father and we are his
children.

We therefore are to pray to him with complete confidence just as children speak to their loving father.

What does this mean?

God's name certainly is holy in itself, but we ask in this prayer that we may keep it holy.

When does this happen?

God's name is hallowed whenever his Word is rightly taught and we as children of God live in harmony with it. Help us to do this, heavenly Father!

But anyone who teaches or lives contrary to the Word of God dishonors God's name among us.
Keep us from doing this, heavenly Father!

What does this mean?

God's kingdom comes indeed without our praying for it, but we ask in this prayer that it may come also to us.

When does this happen?

God's kingdom comes when our heavenly Father gives us his Holy Spirit, so that by his grace we believe his holy Word and live a godly life on earth now and in heaven forever.

The First Petition
Hallowed be thy name.

The Second Petition
Thy kingdom come.

The Third Petition

Thy will be done on earth as it is in heaven.

What does this mean?

The good and gracious will of God is surely done without our prayer, but we ask in this prayer that it may be done also among us.

When does this happen?

God's will is done when he hinders and defeats every evil scheme and purpose of the devil, the world, and our sinful self, which would prevent us from keeping his name holy and would oppose the coming of his kingdom. And his will is done when he strengthens our faith and keeps us firm in his Word as long as we live.

The Fourth Petition

Give us this day our daily bread.

What does this mean?

God gives daily bread, even without our prayer, to all people, though sinful, but we ask in this prayer that he will help us to realize this and to receive our daily bread with thanks.

What is meant by "daily bread"?

Daily bread includes everything needed for this life, such as food and clothing, home and property, work and income, a devoted family, an

orderly community, good
government, favorable
weather, peace and health,
a good name, and true friends
and neighbors.

The Fifth Petition

*And forgive us our tres-
passes, as we forgive those
who trespass against us.*

What does this mean?

We ask in this prayer that our
Father in heaven would not
hold our sins against us and
because of them refuse to
hear our prayer.

And we pray that he would
give us everything by grace,
for we sin every day and
deserve nothing but punishment.

So we on our part will
heartily forgive and
gladly do good to those
who sin against us.

The Sixth Petition

*And lead us not into
temptation.*

What does this mean?

God tempts no one to sin,
but we ask in this prayer that
God would watch over us so
that the devil, the world, and
our sinful self may not
deceive us and draw us into
unbelief, despair, and other
great and shameful sins.

And we pray that even though
we are so tempted we may
still win the final victory.

The Seventh Petition

But deliver us from evil.

What does this mean?

We ask in this inclusive prayer that our heavenly Father would save us from every evil to body and soul, and at our last hour would mercifully take us from the troubles of this world to himself in heaven.

The Doxology

For thine is the kingdom and the power and the glory forever and ever. Amen.

What does "Amen" mean?

Amen means *Yes, it shall be so.*
We say *Amen* because we are certain that such petitions are pleasing to our Father in heaven.
For he himself has commanded us to pray in this way and has promised to hear us.

Part Four
THE SACRAMENT OF BAPTISM

1

What is Baptism?

The sacrament of Baptism is not water only, but it is water used together with God's Word and by his command.

What is this Word?

In Matthew 28 our Lord Jesus Christ says: "Go therefore and make disciples of all nations, baptizing them in the name of the Father and of the Son and of the Holy Spirit."

2

What benefits does God give in Baptism?

> In Baptism God forgives sin,
> delivers from death and the devil,
> and gives everlasting salvation to all who believe
> what he has promised.

What is God's promise?

> In Mark 16 our Lord Jesus Christ says:
> "He who believes and is baptized will be saved;
> but he who does not believe will be condemned."

3

How can water do such great things?

> It is not water that does these things,
> but God's Word with the water and our trust in
> this Word.
> Water by itself is only water,
> but with this Word it is a life-giving water
> which by grace gives the new birth through the
> Holy Spirit.

> St. Paul writes in Titus 3:
> "He saved us . . . in virtue of his own mercy,
> by the washing of regeneration and renewal in
> the Holy Spirit,
> which he poured out upon us richly
> through Jesus Christ our Savior,
> so that we might be justified by his grace
> and become heirs in hope of eternal life.
> The saying is sure."

4

What does Baptism mean for daily living?

> It means that our sinful self, with all its evil deeds
> and desires,

should be drowned through daily repentance;
and that day after day a new self should arise
to live with God in righteousness and purity forever.

St. Paul writes in Romans 6:
"We were buried therefore with him by Baptism
    into death,
so that as Christ was raised from the dead
    by the glory of the Father,
we too might walk in newness of life."

Part Five

THE SACRAMENT OF HOLY COMMUNION

1

What is Holy Communion?
It is the sacrament instituted by Christ himself,
in which he gives us his body and blood
in and with the bread and wine.

What are the Words of Institution?
Our Lord Jesus Christ, in the night in which he
    was betrayed,
took bread; and when he had given thanks,
he broke it and gave it to his disciples,
saying, "Take, eat, this is my body,
    which is given for you;
this do in remembrance of me."

After the same manner also he took the cup after
    supper,
and when he had given thanks,
he gave it to them, saying,
"Drink of it, all of you;
this cup is the new testament in my blood,
which is shed for you, and for many, for the
    remission of sins;
this do, as often as you drink it, in remembrance
    of me."

2

What benefits do we receive from this sacrament?

The benefits of this sacrament are pointed out by
the words,
given and shed for you for the remission of sins.
These words assure us that in the sacrament
we receive forgiveness of sins, life, and salvation.
For where there is forgiveness of sins,
there is also life and salvation.

3

How can eating and drinking do all this?

It is not eating and drinking that does this,
but the words, *given and shed for you for the*
remission of sins.
These words, along with eating and drinking,
are the main thing in the sacrament.
And whoever believes these words
has exactly what they say,
forgiveness of sins.

4

When is a person rightly prepared to received this sacrament?

Fasting and other outward preparations
serve a good purpose.
However, that person is well prepared and
worthy who believes these words,
given and shed for you for the remission of sins.
But anyone who does not believe these words, or
doubts them,
is neither prepared nor worthy,
for the words *for you* require simply
a believing heart.

THE OFFICE OF THE KEYS

What is the "Office of the Keys"?

It is that authority which Christ gave to his church to forgive the sins of those who repent and to declare to those who do not repent that their sins are not forgiven.

What are the words of Christ?

Our Lord Jesus Christ said to his disciples: "Receive the Holy Spirit. If you forgive the sins of any, they are forgiven; if you retain the sins of any, they are retained."—John 20:23

"Truly, I say to you, whatever you bind on earth shall be bound in heaven, and whatever you loose on earth shall be loosed in heaven."—Matthew 18:18

CONFESSION

What is private confession?

Private confession has two parts. First, we make a personal confession of sins to the pastor, and then we receive absolution, which means forgiveness as from God himself. This absolution we should not doubt, but firmly believe that thereby our sins are forgiven before God in heaven.

What sins should we confess?

Before God we should confess that we are guilty of all sins, even those which are not known to us, as we do in the Lord's Prayer. But in private confession, as before the pastor, we should confess only those sins which trouble us in heart and mind.

What are such sins?

We can examine our everyday life according to the Ten Commandments—for example, how we act toward father or mother, son or daughter, husband or wife, or toward the people with whom we work, and so on. We may ask ourselves whether we have been disobedient or unfaithful, bad-tempered or dishonest, or whether we have hurt anyone by word or deed.

How might we confess our sins privately?

We may say that we wish to confess our sins and to receive absolution in God's name. We may begin by saying, "I, a poor sinner, confess before God that I am guilty of many sins." Then we should name the sins that trouble us. We may close the confession with the words, "I repent of all these sins and pray for mercy. I promise to do better with God's help."

What if we are not troubled by any special sins?

We should not torture ourselves with imaginary sins. If we cannot think of any sins to confess (which would hardly ever happen) we need not name any in particular, but may receive absolution because we have already made a general confession to God.

How may we be assured of forgiveness?

The pastor may pronounce the absolution by saying, "By the authority of our Lord Jesus Christ I forgive you your sins in the name of the Father and of the Son and of the Holy Spirit. Amen."

Those who are heavily burdened in conscience the pastor may comfort and encourage with further assurances from God's Word.